Edward Blake

The Overtaxation of Ireland

Edward Blake

The Overtaxation of Ireland

ISBN/EAN: 9783337327613

Printed in Europe, USA, Canada, Australia, Japan

Cover: Foto ©Suzi / pixelio.de

More available books at **www.hansebooks.com**

THE

OVER-TAXATION of IRELAND

———◆———

SPEECH

DELIVERED BY

HON. EDWARD BLAKE, M.P.

(SOUTH LONGFORD)

IN THE

HOUSE OF COMMONS, ON 29TH MARCH, 1897

WITH

Introduction, Index and Tables

PRINTED AND PUBLISHED ON RESOLUTION OF THE
IRISH PARLIAMENTARY PARTY
EDITED BY ALFRED WEBB

Dublin
SEALY, BRYERS AND WALKER
MIDDLE ABBEY STREET

Introduction.

As this speech by the HON. EDWARD BLAKE may fall into the hands of some not fully aware of the circumstances under which it was delivered, it is well to preface it with a few words of explanation.

" At various times " (I quote from the Report hereafter referred to of the Eleven Commissioners) " since the pass-" ing of the Act of Legislative Union between Great " Britain and Ireland, complaints have been made that the " financial arrangements between the two countries were " not satisfactory, or in accordance with the principles of " that Act, and that the resources of Ireland have had to " bear an undue pressure of taxation.

" Inquiries into the truth of these allegations have " frequently been called for, and Committees of the House " of Commons were appointed in 1811, 1812, and 1815, to " investigate the financial results which followed the pass-" ing of the Act of Union. Another Committee of the " House of Commons was appointed in 1864, which took " valuable evidence, collected much documentary informa-" tion, and reported in the year 1865. Nothing practical, " however, followed from the Report of that Committee, " and complaints still continued. In the year 1890 Mr. " Goschen, then Chancellor of the Exchequer, consented " that a further inquiry should be made by another Com-" mittee of the House of Commons. The terms of reference " to that Committee comprised several points, and amongst " others ' the equity of the financial relations in regard to " ' the resources and population of the Three Kingdoms '

" was referred to them. This Committee was appointed too
" late in the session to make any substantial progress, and
" confined itself merely to calling for financial information.
" For various reasons the Committee was not re-appointed,
" and a change of Government taking place in 1892, Mr.
" Gladstone announced his willingness, in connexion with
" the Home Rule Bill of 1893, to have the financial
" relations between the two countries investigated by
" Commission."

The Commissioners, appointed in May, 1894, were:—
The Right Hon. Hugh C. E. Childers (since deceased);
Lord Farrer, Lord Welby, The Right Hon. O'Conor Don,
Sir Robert G. C. Hamilton (since deceased) ; Sir Thomas
Sutherland, K.C.M.G., M.P. ; Sir David Barbour, K.C.S.I ;
The Hon. Edward Blake, M.P. ; Bertram W. Currie, Esq.;
W. A. Hunter, Esq., M.P. ; C. E. Martin, Esq. ; J. E.
Redmond, Esq., M.P. ; Thomas Sexton, Esq., M.P. ;
Henry F. Slattery, Esq. ; G. W. Wolff, Esq., M.P.

The following were the terms of reference :—" To
" inquire into the Financial Relations between Great
" Britain and Ireland, and their relative taxable capacity,
" and to report :—1. Upon what principles of comparison,
" and by the application of what specific standards, the
" relative capacity of Great Britain and Ireland to bear
" taxation may be most equitably determined. 2. What,
" so far as can be ascertained, is the true proportion, under
" the principles and specific standards so determined,
" between the taxable capacity of Great Britain and
" Ireland. 3. The history of the Financial Relations
" between Great Britain and Ireland at and after the
" Legislative Union, the charge for Irish purposes on the
" Imperial Exchequer during that period, and the amount
" of Irish Taxation remaining available for contribution to
" Imperial expenditure ; also the Imperial expenditure to
" which it is considered equitable that Ireland should con-
" tribute."

The Commission reported late last year, and the result

was laid before Parliament in a Blue Book, with accompanying two volumes of evidence. Of the thirteen surviving Commissioners, eleven (The O'Conor Don, Lord Farrer, Lord Welby, Mr. Blake, Mr. Currie, Mr. Hunter, Mr. Martin, Mr. Redmond, Mr. Sexton, Mr. Slattery, Mr. Wolff,) agreed as follows :—

"I. That Great Britain and Ireland must, for the " purpose of this inquiry, be considered as separate entities.

"II. That the Act of Union imposed upon Ireland a " burden which, as events showed, she was unable to bear.

"III. That the increase of taxation laid upon Ireland " between 1853 and 1860 was not justified by the then " existing circumstances.

"IV. That identity of rates of taxation does not " necessarily involve equality of burden.

"V. That whilst the actual tax revenue of Ireland is " about one-eleventh of that of Great Britain the relative " taxable capacity of Ireland is very much smaller, and is " not estimated by any of us as exceeding one-twentieth."

The difference between this one-eleventh and one-twentieth amounts to about £2,750,000 per annum extra taxation.

Separate Reports were made : jointly by The O'Conor Don, Mr. Redmond, Mr. Martin, Mr. Hunter, and Mr. Wolff (28 pages) ; jointly by Lord Farrer, Lord Welby, and Mr. Currie, (22 pages) ; Lord Welby (7 pages); jointly by Mr. Sexton, Mr. Blake and Mr. Slattery (45 pages) ; Mr. Blake, Draft (3 pages) ; Sir David Barbour (18 pages) ; Sir Thomas Sutherland (10 pages) ; and a Draft Report by the deceased Chairman, Mr. Childers (62 pages).

All has been published as a Parliamentary Return [C 8262, 1896] with two volumes of evidence [C 7720, 1895, I and II].

The following general conclusions are arrived at in the able and exhaustive Report of Mr. Sexton :—" Having " regard to the relative taxable capacity of Ireland (1) at " the period of the Union, and (2) at the present time ;

" also to the continual increase of British population, and
" more rapid multiplication of British wealth, contrasted
" with the decline of Irish manufacture and trade after the
" Union, and the great reduction of Irish population, manu-
" facturing industry, and agricultural income since the
" famine, it does not appear that Ireland's fair proportion
" of Imperial revenue collected since the Union amounted
" to more at the utmost than an average of 3 millions per
" annum ; or a total, up to 1894, of about 280 millions.
" The revenue actually raised in Ireland during the period
" of the separate exchequers and 'contributed' since then
" (according to Treasury computations) has amounted to
" about 570 millions, or an average approximately of 6 mil-
" lions a year, being double the amount stated as the fair
" proportion of Ireland in view of her relative capacity."

The clearness with which Ireland's case was educed
from the mass of evidence is largely due to the ability of
Mr. Sexton's examination and cross-examination of the
witnesses, of which, said the Chairman, the Right Hon. The
O'Conor Don, " it would be impossible for me too highly
" to speak." " It may, perhaps," he added, " be invidious
" to mention any other name, but I feel so strongly that
" we are much indebted to another member of the Com-
" mission that I cannot refrain from mentioning him, I
" refer to the Hon. Edward Blake, M.P. To Mr. Blake's
" wise foresight, to his conciliatory address, to his large-
" minded views, and his clearness and precision in enun-
" ciating them, we are much indebted for having secured
" practical unanimity in what is called the Joint Report ;
" and as Chairman of the Commission I feel bound to
" notice the important assistance he has rendered in bring-
" ing about that agreement which has proved of so much
" value."

The Report has excited widespread interest and agitation
in Ireland—all political parties being united on this question. Interrogated regarding their intentions, Government
declined to remedy the grievance exposed, expressed itself

dissatisfied with the inquiry as not covering the whole ground, and announced its intention of appointing a fresh Commission, the terms of reference to which would include a consideration of Imperial expenditure in Ireland, as a set off for excessive taxation. It, however, gave an opportunity for debate ; and Mr. Blake, acting on behalf of the Irish Parliamentary Party, on 29th March, moved the resolution that will be found prefixed to his speech. A three days' debate followed   The motion was negatived by 317 votes to 157.

The speech delivered by Mr. Blake on that occasion was generally felt to be a masterly and comprehensive statement of the Irish case ; and as a mark of their sense of its great and permanent value, and of the service to the National cause rendered by Mr. Blake in making it, it was unanimously resolved at a meeting of the Irish Party—

"That the speech delivered by the Hon. Edward Blake in moving the resolution on the Financial Relations between Great Britain and Ireland be printed and published at the expense of the Party."

At the request of the Party, I have undertaken the task of seeing this speech through the press and arranging for its publication and distribution. It has been to me a congenial duty.

I have ventured to prefix an Index, and, with efficient assistance, to add some Tables illustrative of the argument.

It is to be hoped that this broad statement of Ireland's case will bring home to the minds of many, who have never before examined the question, a realization of the economic injustice under which Ireland has been suffering.

A. W.

DUBLIN, *May,* 1897.

Index.

" *But remember when you have completed your system of impoverishment, that nature still proceeds in her ordinary course, that discontent will increase with misery.*"

—EDMUND BURKE.

" *There is no debt with so much prejudice put off as that of justice.*"—PLUTARCH.

OVER-TAXATION OF IRELAND.

HOUSE OF COMMONS, 29th MARCH, 1897.

HON. EDWARD BLAKE spoke as follows in support of his motion—

"That in the opinion of this House the Report and Proceedings of the Royal Commission on the Financial Relations of Great Britain and Ireland establish the existence of an undue burthen of taxation on Ireland, which constitutes a great grievance to all classes of the Irish community, and makes it the duty of the Government to propose, at an early day, remedial legislation."

Mr. Speaker, I rise to draw attention to the Report of the Royal Commission on the Financial Relations between Great Britain and Ireland, and to state the nature of the Irish case made out by that Report. I am glad to acknowledge that it has been favourably regarded in influential quarters on both sides of the House. But I am not insensible to the fact that there exists on the part of some members an indisposition, perhaps I might say an aversion to the discussion of Irish grievances ; some entertaining a conviction that there is no use in spending more time over Irish affairs, since, whatever is said or done, the people are still unreasonably dissatisfied ; and others cherishing the belief that Ireland is spoiled and favoured, rather than wronged and neglected. I feel too that the argument must be tedious, devoid of dramatic interest, full of wearisome detail. And most of all am I deeply conscious of my own inadequacy for the task which has been imposed upon me.

B

Therefore I very earnestly supplicate the kind indulgence
of the House while I attempt to sustain the motion of which
I have given notice.

Sir, this differs from many former Irish questions. In those
there was not so much as in this a united

Difference
between this
and other
Irish
questions. Ireland. In those the dominating British de-
legation often assumed to be impartial judges,.
disinterested persons, deciding between con-
flicting Irish factions. The Chancellor of the
Exchequer said a while ago that in the discussion of this
matter " a judicial mind " was essential. And the voices of
the Irish Members are little regarded, because they are said
to be parties, and therefore not fit judges in the case.

But who, may I ask. are the other parties ? If we be the
plaintiffs, who are the defendants? You, the British members!
But your position is more powerful, and therefore
more invidious, than ours. We, even if happily united on
this question here as much as in Ireland, would be only
one-seventh of this magisterial bench. You can neutralise
us with near five hundred judges to spare. Thus, in the
decision, we are impotent; you all-powerful. You, then,
are *the* judges ; and we must plead with our adversaries to
give judgment against themselves. On what then can we
depend ? Whence cometh our hope ? We can rest only
on the security declared in 1800 by a great British Minister
to be adequate, when, speaking of this very contingency,.
he said—

"But it has been said. 'What security can you give Ireland for the
performance of the conditions?' If I were asked what security were
necessary, without hesitation I would answer 'None.' The liberality,
the justice, the honour of the people of Great Britain have never yet
been found deficient."

It is for you who speak for Britain to-day to make good
Pitt's words of a century ago.

Sir, I will limit to the utmost my large demand upon
your patience. There are numerous questions, readily dis-
cussible *ad nauseam*, involving economical and statistical
problems, expert opinions, historical and legal views,

columns of figures. By expanding all these, and by dilat-
ing upon the precise extent of the grievance and the
possible kinds of redress, it would be easy to obscure or
sink the issue. I would gladly aim, if possible, rather at
broad outlines and general results, and in some matters
rely on expert authority; but, after all, tedious details are
inevitable.

First let me ask the House to consider the gravity of the
issue; and let me emphasise it by a brief
enumeration of some startling facts, new and
old, collected by the Commission. For almost a
century Britain has ruled Ireland under the
Union. I ask British members to recall the economic conditions of the two islands—the ruling and the ruled. They
should give pause before the dismissal of our plaint.

Economic results of Britain's rule since Union.

Take population. It is a great test, and involves a great
element of strength. At the beginning Ire-
land had five millions against a little over ten
millions in Britain. She has now four and a-half millions,
less by half a million, or 10 per cent. of a loss in the century.
Britain has now thirty-four millions, having increased by
twenty-four millions, or 240 per cent. Had Ireland increased proportionately she would have had over sixteen
millions; her relative loss is eleven and a half millions.
She had half as many: she has little more than one-eighth
of Britain. But even this view is inadequate. Only half a
century ago Ireland had eight and a half millions. She lost
two millions directly and indirectly through the famine;
and since then so many more that, after eliminating the
natural increase, her population has actually diminished by
four millions, or 47 per cent. in half a century, an absolutely
unexampled condition. Britain half a century ago had
twenty millions; she has increased by fourteen millions,
or 70 per cent. A proportionate Irish increase would
make an Irish population of over fourteen millions. Her
relative loss is near ten millions, or 70 per cent. in half a
century.

Population.

Take next the condition of the people. Of this dread-
fully reduced population there are large

Condition
of the
people.

masses whose scale of existence is far below
that of the corresponding masses of Britain ;
while Britain's increased numbers enjoy a
steady and rapid advance in the standard of comfort.

In Britain the scale of living and the margin available
for emergencies make famine unknown and

Famine.

impossible. In Ireland the scale is so
low and the margin so narrow that even a single
bad crop tends in important areas to famine, necessitating
public aid. In 1879-1880, in 1886, in 1891, in 1894, you
were obliged to pass Relief of Distress Acts for Ireland.
In England there is no Congested Districts Board. In
Ireland one-sixth of the country and near one-eighth of
the population are thus dealt with. The average Poor-
Law valuation of the area is £1 0s. 2d. Many equally
poor districts are excluded from the Act. There is painful evidence of chronic penury and want in those parts ;
reports which, if they could be alleged of a British district,
would absolutely appal this House.

Britain imports from Ireland and abroad for her
masses vast quantities of the best foods, in

Food.

addition to what she raises. Ireland raises
great supplies of the best foods, which she is obliged
largely to export to Britain, and to replace by inferior
commodities, Indian corn and American bacon—the best
her poverty-stricken masses can afford to use. Ireland
is, in proportion to population, the fourth meat producer
in the world, but only the sixteenth meat consumer. For
England the conditions are reversed. She is the sixteenth
meat producer, but the fourth meat consumer.

The average Poor-Law valuation of all Ireland is under
£3, about equal to the poorest East London

Poverty.

union. The paupers of Ireland were per
1,000 in 1864, 52 ; of Britain, 49 ; nearly equal proportions.
In 1895 they were in Ireland 95, being nearly doubled ; for

Britain, 26, being almost halved. From equality they have become near 4 to 1 ; an increase, however, partly due to the assimilation of the systems as to out-door relief.

Emigration has been draining from Ireland those in the prime of life. The very young and the very old remain. Thus the absolute and relative efficiency of the population has been lowered.

Physical condition.

Inferior conditions have produced other painful results. The proportion of deaf-mutes is near one-third larger than in England ; of blind, two-fifths ; of lunatics, one-third. And, on the other hand, the proportion of births over deaths is in Ireland less than half that in Britain.

Take manufactures and agriculture. Irish manufactures have largely declined. While between 1841 and 1891 the whole population decreased 42 per cent., the manufacturing population decreased 61 per cent. Now only 27 per cent. of the Irish population is urban. In the same time the manufactures of Britain have immeasurably increased, and now 71 per cent. of her population is urban. The figures are about reversed. Thus, Ireland has become more and more dependent upon the land ; 73 per cent. of her people live in the country, and 64 per cent. are directly dependent upon agriculture. It follows that she has suffered enormously, absolutely and relatively, by the fall in prices, accentuated by the loss of local town markets ; and her gross and net returns from agriculture have been very greatly reduced, involving the loss of a large proportion of her yearly resources. Britain has become more and more independent of agriculture. Under 29 per cent. of her people are rural ; and therefore she has been less affected as a country by the fall in prices ; while agriculture itself has been helped by the wide-spreading urban districts, which have turned large agricultural areas into market gardens, and town supply-farms ; a process which ought to be much accelerated.

Manufactures and Agriculture.

Take commerce. Ireland has hardly any foreign commerce or investments, and a large part of her
yearly income is drained away by absentee
landlords and mortgagees. Britain is still the great
manufacturer, merchant, carrier, and lender of the world,
whose wealth she drains. Though Ireland still has a
population of between one-seventh and one-eighth of
Britain's, the number of her railway passengers is but one-
thirty-seventh; of tons of railway freight, one-seventieth; of
telegrams, one-eighteenth, and of money and postal orders,
one-nineteenth—facts which prove her comparative stag-
nation.

Commerce.

Take resources. Sir Robert Giffen's conclusion is that,
taking into account all circumstances, the
incomes of the wage-earning classes in Ire-
land are, man for man, little more than half those of Great
Britain. The gross income or yearly resources of Ireland
are estimated too highly at 70 millions; those of Britain
too low at 1,400 millions, or twenty-fold. The capital of
Ireland was reckoned in 1820 at 563 millions, or over one-
third that of Britain, which was 1,500 millions. Ireland is
thought now to have 400 millions, or near one-third reduction, and Britain over 10,000 millions, or over seven-
fold increase. Ireland has gone down relatively from over
one-third to under one-twenty-fifth.

Resources.

Sir, these comparisons might be easily multiplied and
enlarged upon, but the bald statements prove
that the conditions of the two islands you
govern are wholly different and increasingly
diverging in the extent of their resources, in the kinds of
their resources, and in their economic circumstances and
interests. They show that your rule has advanced your-
selves, but failed to prosper her. They prove that her
situation demands the just and generous consideration of
the rich and powerful rulers of the weak and poor island
whose destinies you control.

*General
result.*

Let me add this one contrasting fact—that on which our present claim is founded. The one great

The one contrasting fact—Taxation. point in which Britain exhibits a decline and Ireland an advance is in the scale of taxation! In Ireland the taxes on commodities which strike the masses, were per head, in 1790, 4s.; in 1820, 11s.; in 1894, 22s.—they were doubled. In Britain they were, in 1820, 48s.; in 1894, 24s.—they were halved. The Irish taxes which had been under one-fourth have become almost equal, notwithstanding the relative poverty of the country.

Sir, may I deal, before considering our rights under the Union Act, with one cardinal point of

Maximum estimate of Relative Taxable Capacity. Report. economic fact; the relative taxable capacity of the two islands, as contrasted with their actual taxation. For the purposes of this debate it is enough to show the maximum estimate of Ireland's relative capacity, reached by any one of twelve out of thirteen commissioners. The Joint Report finds that—

"While the actual tax revenue of Ireland is about one-eleventh of that of Britain, the relative taxable capacity of Ireland is very much smaller, and is not estimated by any of us to exceed one-twentieth."

This conclusion was reached after two years' examination and consideration by eminent experts,

Personnel of British section of Commission. financiers, statisticians, and Treasury officials. Let me, because of the imputation of bias, leave out all the Irish members, though some of them, at any rate, ought to count in this question. Let me consider the British members only, who also, by the same reasoning, may have been unconsciously biassed against us. It was reached substantially by Mr. Childers, the first chairman, a distinguished economist and financier, an ex-Chancellor of the Exchequer, a man retired from party politics, who devoted the last years of his life to this great public service, in the discharge of which he died. It was reached by Lords Farrer and Welby, who had filled the highest posts in the British Treasury, and in the Board of

Trade—posts demanding and developing the qualities most required for the work ; and whose public services had been rewarded by seats in the Upper Chamber, which was honoured and strengthened by their accession to its ranks. It was reached by the late Mr. Currie, a man of the highest reputation in these walks, who had proved his powers in other posts ; and by Professor Hunter, a late colleague of ours, whose brain-power, knowledge, and industry are well-known here. It was reached substantially by Sir David Barbour, dissentient on other grounds, whose distinguished career abroad may, perhaps, permit him to be admitted as impartial, though marked by Irish birth. There remains just one British member; perhaps the Chancellor of the Exchequer would say *the* just one—a colleague of ours who does not give assent, proceeding on other lines, but, not as I understand, negativing the conclusion. It has indeed been said that even these British members are tainted, too, because they are favourers of Home Rule. But this is not now a question, though you may make it one, of Home Rule. The claim to Home Rule is made on other grounds. It is an absurd contention (as has been shown by the hon. member for Plymouth, whose sympathetic treatment of our case I gladly acknowledge) that such opinions could vitiate their judgment on this economic question. Then you must, as I submit, give great weight to the conclusions of that body of men, experts, but of like passions with ours, and subject to the same infirmities, who have yet found against themselves and you. It was reached on the evidence of Sir Robert Giffen and Sir Edward Hamilton, and others, great British public servants—the one the able head of the Treasury and the other an economist and statistician of eminent repute, heightened by his display on this occasion. It was reached after collecting, weighing, and sifting all information suggested from every quarter, and valuing and applying all tests—population, imports and exports, consumption of duty-paid goods, consumption of commodities of primary use, assessment of death duties, assessment of income tax, other incomes and wages, yearly wealth, aggregate production, capital, comparative progress of capacity, relative effects of fiscal policy, and so on, with statistical facts too numerous to name.

It was reached after examination of the principles of taxation and their application, including some which made a serious difference amongst us, mainly because some of us thought that the gross income was relatively smaller, and that a larger application was needed of the principles of equality of sacrifice, of deduction of a subsistence allowance, and of the relative taxable weakness of a poor as compared with a wealthy country. Some of us believed, and now believe, that a just application of these principles would show the Irish relative capacity much less, and her taxable surplus almost exhausted, while the British is hardly touched. We saw an Irish surplus over living allowance of perhaps fifteen millions mainly abstracted by taxation, and a British surplus of perhaps eleven hundred millions less than tithed by taxation. We saw the Irish relative taxable capacity steadily diminishing. We thought, in accordance with Sir Robert Giffen, that a far lower proportion would be true, and also that a maximum contribution should be fixed so as to meet the proved danger of excessively increased expenditure. I quite agree that a rigorous application of these figures and principles is not to be hoped for yet. It still is true that—

Maximum too high.

"To him that hath shall be given, and he shall have more abundantly; and from him that hath not shall be taken away even that which he hath."

But a nearer approach should be made ; and I hope some day to maintain this view in this place. Meantime, I ask you to remember that this is stated only as a maximum. Sir Edward Hamilton himself, towards the close of the inquiry, put the relation of resources as one twenty-second apart, as I understand, from the question of subsistence allowance, and Lord Farrer has lately, in another place, declared his conviction to be that the maximum named is too high. For my present purpose, this is enough and more than enough. It so far proves a great

Enormous Over-Taxation proved.

disproportion—so far establishes a substantial grievance—so far calls for a remedy. I would only ask you to remember that the contribution of Ireland is between one-eleventh and one-twelfth, or nearly twice her maximum relative taxable capacity, and thus reaches a minimum excess of two and three-quarter millions. As I have said, on the question of precise degree the Commission was divided. All the facts and arguments are now before the Government, which should propose a decision to be settled some other day on broad lines by Parliamentary adjustment and compromise. I cannot then accept this as the just estimate; I ask you to accept it only as a maximum. Indeed, I am not sure that this proposition is now disputed. It takes me only part of the way in my argument; but I strongly argue that by itself it creates an urgent case for relief on the grounds of fair play and generous consideration due from the strong to the weak.

But, sir, the case of Ireland stands higher. It stands upon treaty and justice, equity and right.

True basis of Ireland's Case. Report.

Ireland has been found by the Commission entitled to separate consideration as a fiscal entity in this question of contribution; and the finding is of weight. This is, however, not a question especially for experts. It is based on historical, legal, and equitable considerations, peculiarly for the final decision of this House, and I must ask your patience while I briefly state its grounds.

In 1782, Ireland had partly emerged from that condition of servitude as to her trade and manufactures

History— 1782 to 1800. Grattan's Parliament.

described in 1785 in wounding words by Pitt, adding "Ireland had been made completely subservient to the interests and opulence of Great Britain;" and further, "Such a system, however necessary it might be to the partial benefit of districts in Britain, promoted not the real strength and prosperity of the Empire." From 1782 to 1800 Ireland had a measure of independence, though under a defective constitution. During the first ten years there was peace. The country, though poor, was improving ; manufactures, productions, and exports expanded ; the establishments were moderate; the taxation was one million, equal to 4s. a head, all on consumption ; and it met the expenditure. Then came the French war, followed by the Rebellion, after which a large army was planted on the country during the negotiations for the Union. These calamities had, by 1800, raised the taxation to two and a-half millions, or 10s. a head. There was a deficiency of over sixteen millions—ten millions for the war ; six millions for the Rebellion and armed occupation. To meet this a debt of twenty-eight millions had been created, the charge for which was one and a-quarter millions. This condition was, of course, abnormal and temporary. The taxation of Britain at the same time, of which two-thirds was upon consumption, was £3 a head, or six-fold that of Ireland.

Then came the proposals for Union. They excited alarm at the danger of over-taxation of Ireland. Speaker Foster, and other Irish members, in language which sounds prophetic now, anticipated the sad future. These alarms it was necessary to soothe.

1800. Union Proposals.

There was no pretence that Ireland was able to bear the British rate of taxation. Her absolute and relative poverty was acknowledged, and calculations were made professing to show the relative resources and to fix the just proportion of contribution of each country to the common burden to be assumed by the United Kingdom. The bases were unsound, narrow, defective, now exploded ; and, besides, they included some unfit Irish, and excluded

British Acknowledgments in Union Debates' Quota System.

some proper British elements of calculation. The result
was an erroneous estimate of relative taxable capacity of
two to fifteen. Mark that the population was one to two;
the quota, one to seven and a-half. The justice of the estimate was disputed. The Irish Lords protested, calculating
that one to eighteen or twenty was the truth ; and they
were justified by the event. The principle of proportionate
contribution was sound ; but its application was false, and
its results were ruinous.

It was thought possible that a change might be made later
allowing equal and indiscriminate taxation,
subject to abatements and exemptions for
Ireland. The main difficulty present to
men's minds was the debt. Apparently the
promoters contended that the leading end, namely—
contribution according to resources—could be accom-
plished by the alternative arrangement. But it is clear
that this was not absolutely held, for in April, 1800, Pitt
said—

*Indiscrimi-
nate
Taxation
system.*

> " It were a consummation much to be wished that the finances of
> both countries were so nearly alike that the systems of both could be
> identified. But as, from the different proportions of debt, different
> stages of civilisation and commerce, and the different wealth of the
> nations, that desirable object is rendered impracticable for some time
> to come,"

And so on. Thus there was a clear acknowledgment of
the elements of our case—the materiality of
the differences in civilisation, commerce, and
wealth of the nations. The British professions
were all against any increase of Irish burdens. Pitt assured the House—

*Pitt's
professions.*

> " That the Union was not sought from a pecuniary motive ; "
> " it must infuse a large portion of wealth into Ireland, and supply
> its want of industry and capital ; " " there was no ground for the
> apprehension that Britain would tax Ireland more heavily," " or that
> Ireland would be subject to an increase of taxes or to a load of debt ; "
> " the contribution to be imposed on Ireland would not be greater
> than her own present necessary expenses ; " " Ireland would continue
> to contribute in its accustomed proportion ; " and that " one of the

objects of the Act was to ensure that Ireland should never be taxed but in proportion as we tax ourselves."

Castlereagh's professions.

Viscount Castlereagh in the Irish House said the same. He stated that the plan of revision—

" Gave to Ireland the utmost possible security that she could not be taxed beyond the measure of her comparative ability, and the ratio of her contribution must ever correspond with her relative wealth and prosperity."

He, however, suggested that if indiscriminate taxation were adopted it would have this effect, saying that—

" By no means whatsoever could the kingdoms be made to contribute so strictly according to their means as being subject to the same taxes, equally bearing on the great objects of taxation in both countries."

Abatements and Exemptions.

Thus this suggestion was not to defeat but to maintain the principle of proportionate contribution of the two countries, and, therefore, it was coupled with appropriate security, being made—

" Subject to abatements and exemptions in Ireland and Scotland, which circumstances might from time to time demand."

On this provision, Castlereagh said—

" While Ireland is thus secured against any injustice in substituting a system of common taxes in lieu of proportionate contribution, the Union Parliament will always be able to make abatements in Ireland, as the Parliament of Great Britain has always done in Scotland since the Union, when from local circumstances the high duty cannot be levied without either rendering the revenue unproductive or pressing too hard upon the poorer classes."

Ireland a Separate Taxable entity always.

Mark these words. They explode the idea that the comparative poverty of the poorer classes in Ireland is to be ignored. It is to be recognised. The individuality of the country, the separate entity, so to speak, is in this respect, maintained. And indeed it is absurd to argue that a country full of contrasts with Britain in all respects, for which you are every day legislating separately, whose whole body of law is different from yours, should be in this matter, in which also its distinctions are fundamental, recognised and increasing, treated as one with you.

Pitt, indeed, could not decline to recognise the rule we invoke as between a poor and a rich country, for in 1785 he said, as to these two islands—

Subsistence Allowance.

"The smallest burden on a poor country was to be considered when compared with those of a rich one, by no means in proportion to the several abilities, for if one country exceeded another in wealth, population and established commerce, even in a proportion of two to one, he was nearly convinced that that country would be able to bear near ten times the burden that the other would be equal to."

The reason is that in order to pay taxes we must live; and that therefore a subsistence allowance must be made; and even the margin after that allowance cannot be heavily touched without disaster. Some economists think that fifteen per cent. is the extreme point on an average; and, of course, the narrower the margin, the sooner the extreme point would be reached. These considerations show that it was intended to secure and maintain a due recognition of the inferior capacity of Ireland, as a country, so long as that inferiority existed; first by the creation and revision of the quota; and later, if the other plan were adopted, by due consideration in the levying, and due exemptions and abatements from the taxes.

If, then, it be possible so to read the Act it ought to be so read. Sir, it is not only possible but inevitable. Look at the Union Act, as quoted in Mr. Childers' Report. The seventh article, after providing separately for the debt, enacts—

Union Act: Taxation by Quota.

"That for twenty years the contribution of Britain and Ireland respectively towards the expenditure of the United Kingdom shall be defrayed in the proportion of fifteen parts for Britain and two parts for Ireland; and at the expiration of twenty years the future expenditure of the United Kingdom shall be defrayed in such proportion as Parliament shall deem just and reasonable—(1) on comparison of imports and exports; (2) on comparison of consumption of beer, spirits, sugar, wine, tea, tobacco, and malt; (3) or according to the aggregate proportion of both the above comparisons; (4) or on comparison of income, in case a general like income tax was established. The Parliament was afterwards to proceed in like manner to revise and fix the proportion of burdens at intervals of from twenty to seven years, and the fixed proportion was to be raised in each country by such taxation in that country as Parliament deemed fit."

So far all is quota ; and all is clear. Then the Act provides that—

Union Act : Indiscriminate Taxation.   "(1) If, at any future day, the separate debt of each country be liquidated or reach equal proportions, and (2) if it shall appear to Parliament that the respective circumstances of the two countries will thenceforth admit of their contributing indiscriminately by equal taxes imposed on the same articles in each, to the future expenditure of the United Kingdom, it shall be competent to Parliament to declare that all future expenditure and the debt charge shall be so defrayed indiscriminately and by equal taxes imposed on the same articles in each country ; and thenceforth from time to time, as circumstances may require, to impose and apply such taxes accordingly, subject only to such abatements and exemptions in Ireland and in that part of Great Britain called Scotland, as circumstances may appear from time to time to demand."

The principle of comparative National Capacity continues still.   Note that it was not on the sole condition of the attainment of the quota by the debt, but also on the determination of Parliament that "the circumstances of the two countries would admit of it," that the change could take place. And thus, even thereafter, the principle of regulating the contribution by national circumstances remained. Note again that even if the change did take effect, yet the imposition of equal taxes on the same articles was subject in Ireland, though not in any English county, to abatements and exemptions. It was recognised therefore that the plan might not produce the stipulated result, which was still intended, of contribution according to ability; and a remedy was provided for all time. I implore you not to minimise that remedy! This safeguard against national injustice under the indiscriminate system was designed to preserve to Ireland substantially the same immunities. Does anyone pretend that it was designed that her condition should be injuriously affected by the later change? Could the Act of Union have been carried on any such suggestion ?

Ireland is not placed in the position of an English county. You ask why should not Wiltshire or East London complain. Some answers are—They have not our clause : they have no distinctive position : they are protected as parts of the ruling island.

Ireland not an English county.

It is thus clear that Ireland has always been entitled to claim that she should be taxed by the United Kingdom Parliament only in substantial proportion to her relative taxable capacity, and it is clear also that, regard being had to that relative capacity, she has been overtaxed by this Parliament.

Result.

Well, Sir, one would say the question is ended! But it is now argued that this is only half the issue ; that there is a question of the application of United Kingdom taxation ; that it is to be divided into four sets of estimates; one for England, one for Scotland, one for Ireland, and one for the United Kingdom ; that the contribution of each of the three countries is to be charged first with its own estimate ; that the obligation to proportionate contribution applies only to the newly proposed United Kingdom estimate ; and therefore that it is only in respect to the balance available for this new and separate estimate that any question of overtaxation can arise. It is to the recognition and application of this new principle that the proposed Commission is mainly directed ; and against that proposal we protest.

Proposed division of Expenditure.

The First Lord of the Treasury said at Manchester, on the eve of the session, that those who argue that Ireland's capacity is one-twenty-first are, necessarily committed to the view that she should pay one-twenty-first to what he is pleased to call Imperial objects; and he argued that the expenditure of the Imperial Parliament is to be divided into three amounts— one to be debited to Britain, one to Ireland, and one to remain as the true Imperial Budget, in respect of which latter alone, no matter what the results of the other accounts.

Mr. Balfour at Manchester.

her taxable proportion is to be paid by Ireland. This he called "clear and logical"; and he declared that the result of this method would be to show that Ireland was not over-taxed, but under-taxed by the present system. And it is to establish this result that he intends the new Commission.

Sir, I will show later the circumstances under which this novel and schismatical doctrine was pro-

The Union Act allows no division of Expenditure.

mulgated, and is now advanced, and its extraordinary, far-reaching, and separatist consequences, wholly opposed to the general conception of Unionist policy. And I will then deal with certain exceptional provisions which demand separate consideration. At present I deal with the contention only in its general aspect and on the basis of the treaty, in order to relieve the House from recurrence to that fundamental instrument. Now, what support does the general contention derive from this, the only effective quarter? None! Absolutely none! The treaty rightly regards all expenditure by the Parliament of the United Kingdom as United Kingdom expenditure. Its basis is that all expenditure decided on by that Parliament, as in its view required, wherever or of whatever nature, without regard to the locality in which it is made, shall form one total, to be contributed to by each country according to its relative taxable capacity. The United Parliament, in which Britain had an overwhelming majority, had power to fix the objects and the scale of expenditure. Ireland could not lay burdens on Britain, or vote herself one necessary shilling. Britain could lay burdens on Ireland, and could refuse to vote her an unnecessary shilling. The dread of Ireland was that she might be over-taxed and under-supplied; and the Treaty was framed to meet this apprehension. You may say—"What! is Britain to pay and Ireland to spend?" Not so. The United Kingdom is to expend on objects which practically the British majority decides are proper, in whatever part of the kingdom the expenditure may take place, and to whatever extent Par-

c

liament may think necessary. And, to the aggregate
expenditure so settled, each country is to contribute in
proportion to its capacity. But you, the Unionists, are
now arguing that the expenditure is in effect federal, and
must be subject to separate accounts!

Let me recur to the Treaty to demonstrate the truth.
It contains one, and but one, provision for

Union Act
provisions for
Expenditure. separate contribution by each country, namely,
to the debt charge ; and this was established
in justice to Ireland, because her debt was so
much lighter that to consolidate the debt would have
involved a disproportionate burden. But this exception
from the general rule marks more clearly, in reason and
in law, that in all other matters there was to be no separate
accounting. It goes on to provide for the defrayal of the

"Expenditure of the United Kingdom"

in the quota proportions, and for the defrayal, after twenty
years, of—

"the future expenditure of the United Kingdom (other than the
interest and charge of the debt to which either country shall be
separately liable)"

in proportions to be ascertained as provided. Thus the
whole expenditure of the United Kingdom, apart from
the debt charges, was so to be defrayed. But the Act lays
down that—

" For defraying the said expenditure, according to the rules above
laid down, the revenues of Ireland shall hereafter constitute a consolidated fund which shall be charged in the first instance with the interest
and sinking fund of the debt of Ireland, and the remainder shall be
applied towards defraying the proportion of the expenditure of the
United Kingdom to which Ireland may be liable in each year."

It provides that the proportion of the contribution to
which Britain and Ireland would be liable shall be raised
by such taxes in each country as the Parliament of the
United Kingdom shall determine, with a provision against
certain increases in Irish duties. It then enacts that—

" If at the end of any year any surplus shall accrue from the revenues
of Ireland, after defraying the interest and sinking fund and the pro-

portion of the contributions and separate charges to which Ireland shall then be liable, taxes shall be taken off to the amount of such surplus, or the surplus shall be applied by the Parliament of the United Kingdom to local purposes in Ireland, or to make good any deficiency in the Irish revenue in time of peace, or to be invested to accumulate for the benefit of Ireland in time of war."

It is thus clearly shown by the specific appropriation of the whole revenues of Ireland that there is no place whatever for the proposed plan. Every shilling to be raised from her is appropriated ; and no possibility exists of such an application as is now suggested. Again, the House will remark the provision for the application of a surplus to local purposes in Ireland. It is not every expenditure in Ireland that is local; the place alone does not make it " local ;" the purpose itself must also be local. The Act also provides for the application for twenty years "to local purposes in Ireland" (repeating the same phrase) to be decided by the Parliament of the United Kingdom, of a sum equal to the average grants by the Irish Parliament for the prior six years in premiums for the internal encouragement of agriculture or manufactures, or for the maintenance of institutions for pious and charitable purposes. Now, Sir, it seems to me too clear for argument that no such principle as is now set up was contemplated or agreed to at the Union under the quota system. And I need not say that no such practice was attempted.

But the Act, when providing for a possible change to indiscriminate taxation, only provides a new method for supplying the same expenditure, on the same principle of just contribution, and contains no hint of authority for any different dealing. It provides for this possible change only—

No change under common taxation.

"If it shall appear to Parliament that the respective circumstances of the two countries will admit of their contributing indiscriminately to the future expenditure of the United Kingdom."

It enacts that in that case—

"All future expenses thenceforth to be incurred "

shall be defrayed accordingly, subject to abatements and

exemptions. This is the same expenditure, provided for according to the same general principle, namely, relative resources, by another method. It introduces no further change. Under the new idea the protection of Ireland would be quite illusory, for she might be taxed beyond the quota by the United Kingdom Parliament, which might make provision for large expenditure in Ireland, forming a prior charge on the quota. How could this be met, save by extra taxation? Yet the quota limit was provided to meet all taxation.

Now, Sir, as this is a cardinal point, I fear I must trouble the House with the views of that great majority of the Commissioners who, by separate yet accordant reports, reached my conclusion. Mr. Childers says :—

The Reports on this head.

"We think that the nature of public expenditure in Ireland and the possibility of reducing it would be a very proper subject for a separate inquiry. It does not, however, seem that, because the cost of central administration in Ireland is greater relatively to population and wealth than it is in Great Britain, this, by itself, is any reason why the people of Ireland should contribute to the public revenue a share in excess of her relative wealth." "It was, in our opinion, the clear intention of the promoters of the Act of Union that so far as related to taxation, or the raising of revenue (whether contributing, as she did, according to a certain ratio till 1817, or whether, as subsequently, by way of indiscriminate taxation, subject to exemptions), Ireland should have a distinct position and a separate consideration. But it was equally their intention that all expense, including no less that upon civil government in Ireland than that upon the army and navy, should be in common or Imperial. It was never intended that the ratio of contribution or the extent of the exemptions and abatements (as the case might be) should be affected by the consideration of the relative cost of administration in each of the three countries. We think that while the legislative and fiscal Union between the kingdom remains this way of treating the matter must hold good."

The O'Conor Don and Messrs. Redmond, Hunter, Martin, and Wolf say in substance :—

"The division of the Imperial expenditure into three parts—one for local purposes in Great Britain, one for local purposes in Ireland, and one for Imperial purposes, is a distinction of quite modern creation. It was not thought of at the time of the Act of Union. It is quite clear, according to the provisions of that Act, that the Imperial expenditure to which Ireland was to contribute under that Act included all civil government expenditure, no matter in what part of the United

Kingdom it took place. Nothing can be clearer than Mr. Pitt's and Lord Castlereagh's declarations on this point, and it is not denied by Sir Edward Hamilton that if the provisions of the Act of Union were still in force Imperial expenditure should be treated as a whole, and could not be split up in the way he suggests. This distinction was not thought of either at the time of the amalgamation of the Exchequers, or when Irish taxation was increased, or in the Irish Taxation Committee of 1864. In truth, at those times, it would not have served as a defence, for the account was all the other way, and the adoption of this principle would have proved Ireland a creditor."

Mr. Sexton and Messrs. Slattery and Blake say in substance :—

"Ireland, under the Treaty of Union, is, and must be regarded as, a separate country for the purpose of taxation. This is evident by the system of proportional taxation. Yet Lord Castlereagh, in moving the article, dwelt on the sacrifice to be made by Great Britain and the advantage to be gained by Ireland, and in proof of this advantage declared that—'If the proportion of expenditure be rightly fixed and ascertained upon just principles for every part of the empire it is immaterial to Great Britain where the expenditure takes place.' The principle thus enunciated, contribution according to relative means, expenditure as required, and without regard to limit of contribution, is the principle of the Treaty. Thus Ireland is to contribute her whole revenue to the whole revenue of the United Kingdom—not part of it to meet one set of charges and the rest to defray another ; nor has the amount of Imperial expenditure any effect or bearing on the question of the amount which her circumstances, compared to those of Britain, enable her to contribute to the common exchequer. The Imperial Parliament secured the power and accepted the duty of administering Irish affairs on the covenant that the taxation of Ireland should not be in excess of her relative resources. The violation of this covenant cannot be justified or excused by a reference to the kind of expenditure in Ireland which the Imperial Parliament, in the discharge of its assumed duty, has thought it necessary or proper to incur."

It appears from the evidence that the late Sir Robert Hamilton was of the same opinion. There are then ten Commissioners, including three British Commissioners— Messrs. Childers, Hamilton, and Hunter—who have taken this position. And Lords Farrer and Welby and Mr. Currie, while—pressed, as I understand, by certain special cases—they are

"unable to admit the general principle that local expenditure which is sanctioned by the Imperial Parliament must be regarded as Imperial expenditure,"

think that

"there is both truth and value in the contrary allegations [which

they set out] if these be confined to the support of the argument that
we cannot, in taking an account between the two countries, justly set
off the whole or the greater part of this expenditure against the over-
taxation of Ireland."

And thus there is, to a very large extent, unanimity on
this head. I will deal later with the special cases referred
to. At present I ask the House to agree that in the
Treaty there is no ground for the general contention that
expenditure in Ireland by the United Kingdom Parliament is to be separately borne by Ireland.

Well, Sir, the Union was consummated. The long war
followed at enormous cost. Irish taxation was
raised from under three millions in 1800 to six
millions in 1817. The Select Committee of
1811 reported serious falls in the Irish revenue
in several periods, caused by a lessened yield, concurrently
with doubled and trebled duties. The Select Committee
of 1817 found that Ireland had advanced in permanent
taxation faster than Britain ; for while Britain's permanent
taxation had been raised in the proportion of $16\frac{1}{2}$ to 10,
and her whole revenue, including war taxes, as $21\frac{1}{4}$ to 10,
Irish taxation had been raised as 23 to 10. The bulk of
the Irish increase was on the consumption of the masses
which was taxed to and beyond the highest productive
point. Yet Ireland could not meet the quota. Her debt
was increased by 84 millions as against a British increase
of 291 millions, or as 1 to $3\frac{1}{2}$.

*History—
1800 to 1817.
The quota
excessive.*

Thus the predictions of the Union-makers were falsified
by the event. The Irish Lords' protest against
the Union Act sounds like a prophecy. They
had protested—

*Predictions of
Union makers
falsified.*

" Because, when we compare the relative abilities of Great Britain
and Ireland, we find the contributions to be paid by the two kingdoms to the expenses of the new Empire most unequally adjusted ;
that the share of 2-17ths fixed upon us as the proportion to be paid
by Ireland is far beyond what her resources will enable her to discharge. Should Ireland undertake to pay more than she shall be
able to answer, the act will be irrevocable, and the necessary consequences will be a gradual diminution of her capital, the decline of her

trade, a failure in the produce of her taxes, and, finally her total bankruptcy.'

The quota was excessive! Some of the Commissioners think it was because the rate was too high ; others because the war was too costly ; others for both these reasons. But there is practical unanimity in the finding that—

"The Act of Union imposed on Ireland a burden which, as events showed, she was unable to bear."

This finding I ask the House to assent to ; and to remember that this was the beginning of the evil.

This first experience demonstrates the truth of the view that there should be some limitation to the call which, under such a union, the richer may make on the poorer nation. A joint expenditure, the proportion of which, though heavy, may be tolerable on a lower scale of joint expense, becomes intolerable to the poorer nation when the scale is raised, while it may be no more than heavy, and quite tolerable still, to the richer nation. Another illustration has been given by the results of the very latest statements as between Ireland and Britain, which show that while Ireland's contribution is larger than ever, the disproportionate excess contributed by Britain has apparently lessened for the year the Irish grievance !

Need of limitation of contribution.

By this road Ireland approached a bankruptcy due to the unjust quota fixed by the Union Act, and one would have thought it the fairest course to anticipate by three years the stipulated term, and to revise the quota at once. But by this road, though through a reversed process, the debts had come into quota proportion, and this opportunity was used to bring the other plan into force. For lack of time I pass over, however serious, the irregular dealings with the joint and separate debts, though I think they were contrary to the Act, and a violation of the agreement, and did not form a legal basis of action.

New plan adopted. Common taxation.

The plan was proposed as the simplest means of dealing with the debt, and it is perfectly clear that there was no intention at that time of actually levying indiscriminate taxation. On the contrary, Lord Liverpool, then Prime Minister, in contemplation of the measure, said in 1815:—

No intention of actually levying common taxes. Abatements and exemptions.

"He trusted that when the two Treasuries of Great Britain and Ireland should be consolidated, such a measure, arranged with due caution, would be found exceedingly advantageous to all parties, and that the Irish public would benefit by its operation. Care would, no doubt, be taken in regulating the taxation to pay due regard to local circumstances, and that the principle of the measure in contemplation should be equally fair to Great Britain and Ireland."

And Mr. Vesey Fitzgerald, the Irish Chancellor, said in reference to the results of the consolidation:—

"I do not fear that Parliament will ever declare the competency of Ireland to bear the entire weight of that taxation which the wealth and resources of England enable her to support, without reference to those considerations upon which alone Ireland should be exempted from those burthens which are laid upon all other subjects of the United Kingdom. The power of that exemption is specially reserved to Parliament by the Act of Union."

After the requisite preliminaries, on the 1st July, 1816, the Bill consolidating the debts and revenues became law. But in these proceedings twice reappears the Union Act provision as to abatements and exemptions. The extraordinary declaration that—

1816. Consolidation Act.

"The circumstances will admit of indiscrimate taxation,"

is itself made,

"subject to such particular abatements and exemptions in Ireland and Scotland as circumstances may from time to time appear to demand."

The declaration of expediency provides for the imposition of common taxation subject to abatements and exemptions in the same terms. Thus the Union Act provision has never lost its force. It was long acted on substantially; it is acted on to some extent to-day.

Sir, may I now briefly state the course of taxation from
1817 to 1860. There was, up to 1853, no sub-
Course of   stantial assimilation. Twenty millions of the
taxation, 1817
to 1860.   taxation of Britain was not imposed on Ireland.
But though peace had been restored, and the
expenditure of the United Kingdom enormously lessened,
the Irish taxation, already shown to be excessive, was
retained, while great remissions were made of the British
war taxes.

The policy of freeing the burdens on manufactures by
abolishing the taxes on materials and on food
Free trade.   supplies was evolved and prosecuted. To this
Effect on
Britain.   new end Peel, in 1842 and in 1845, renewed
the British income tax, originally a war tax.
But it was not extended to Ireland, on the grounds that it
had never existed there ; that there was no machinery for
its collection ; and that, as Britain would derive by far the
greater advantage from the policy, it was but fair that she
should bear the tax.   In fact, five and a-half millions of
taxation thus imposed on Britain enabled the remission
of twelve millions to Britain. This was a good and fair
argument. But I ask the House to note the recognition
of the separateness, and of the diverse conditions, and of
the different effects on different countries of a common
system which it involves. I wish these sound views had
continued to prevail. The general result was to lighten
British burdens, directly and indirectly, and to promote
enormously her commerce and manufactures, her wealth
and population—in short, her tax-paying power.

The policy as to free food supplies was, of course, precipi-
tated by the Irish famine, when her people
Free Trade :   died of hunger, while large quantities of food
Effect
on Ireland.   were being exported from the country to pay
rents. Ireland, whose manufactures had nearly
perished, and were decaying still, derived no such gains as
Britain, while she lost the advantage of preference in the
British markets for her agricultural produce. It is worth

remarking that the conditions of foreign production and of transport and other circumstances for many years retarded the disadvantages to the agricultural interest; and it is only within recent years, as to grain, and a still shorter period, as to meat, that it has experienced the full effects of the change. The economic condition of Ireland was very bad. The great famine inflicted on her a frightful blow, and thus her relative inferiority was increased.

I must not enter into details; but few of the changes in her taxation were directly very adverse to Ireland, save the tobacco taxes, until 1853; when Mr. Gladstone, in furtherance of Peel's fiscal policy, proposed the extension for a limited term of the Income Tax to Ireland. He acknowledged the greater poverty of the masses, but contended that this did not exempt the wealthy from their obligation—an argument valid as to the adjustment between the classes of the Irish people of the payment of her total share, but fallacious as a justification of an increase of that total. As a set-off, he wiped out the famine advance debt of four millions, two millions of which had been reported by the Lords' Committee as properly a grant. But the temporary Income Tax was made permanent, and the burden has enormously outweighed the boon.

Income Tax imposed on Ireland.

A little later Mr. Gladstone began the raising of the spirit duties, on the plea that it was no part of an Irishman's rights to get drunk cheaper than an Englishman. I will have to show later on how this works in practice. The spirit duties were raised at intervals, and were equalised by Mr. Disraeli in 1859.

Spirit Duties raised in Ireland.

The result of these operations was to increase the Irish taxation by more than two millions, or over 40 per cent. Thus, while the average revenue of Britain was no more than during the war at the beginning of the century, her population and wealth had greatly increased, and so her taxation was

General results: Unjustifiable increase.

much lightened. But the average revenue of Ireland had been raised over a third, and it was borne by a diminishing population out of contracting means. This dreadful change took place while Ireland was staggering under the blow of the famine, the after effects of which were accentuated by the added burdens. The British rate of taxation through duties on commodities was—in 1820, £2 8s. 7d.; in 1860, £1 11s. 7d.: the Irish rate was 11s. and £1 0s. 7d. The taxation of the wealthier country had been greatly diminished, that of the poorer enormously increased. The Joint Report finds that—

"The increase of taxation laid upon Ireland between 1853 and 1860 was not justified by the then existing circumstances."

The separate reports practically agree. It is this general verdict which I ask the House to endorse and to effectuate to-day.

I must touch briefly upon what has happened since. Complete assimilation has not yet been attempted. There are some exemptions still. Much cry has been made about four millions of British taxation not imposed on Ireland. Its imposition would not affect the masses of that community; it is mainly on wealth; and its estimated yield, if imposed on Ireland, would be only £150,000, or in the proportion of one twenty-seventh.

Course of Taxation since 1860.

Since 1860 the chief change in Irish burdens has been in the increase of local rates. These stood in 1840 at £1,500,000, or 3s. a head; in 1861, at £1,875,000, or 6s. 5d. a head; in 1893, at £3,700,000, or 15s. 8d. a head; thus increasing steadily, notwithstanding certain grants from Imperial taxation in aid of local rates, to a present total of nearly four millions. The spending authorities are mainly grand juries and guardians—the one entirely and the other largely composed of appointed members; and naturally extravagance, mismanagement, and partiality are complained of.

Irish local rates.

The general effect of the British fiscal policy has been to abolish nearly all duties on raw materials and food, and substituting direct taxation on income and property, and heavy duties on three or four articles of wide and general consumption. These are the articles most largely consumed in Ireland ; while the articles freed were so freed mainly for the benefit of Britain. Now, I am not for a moment objecting to the adoption of Free Trade, or of any other policy advantageous to the interests of the great bulk of the United Kingdom ; but I do emphatically aver that the relative advantages and disadvantages ensuing to each country, affecting as they do the relative taxable power of each, must be considered.

General effect of fiscal policy.

Now, the tax revenue of Ireland in 1820 was 14s. 5d. per head ; in 1894, 28s. 10d. ; or twice as great. That of Britain was, in the earlier year, £3 10s. 3d. ; in the later, £2 4s. 10d., or nearly one-third less. The total taxation in Ireland, including rates, had largely increased in 1850, and was then £1 per head ; in 1880, £2 ; in 1894, £2 8s. 10d.; now, £2 11s. 11d. Her tax revenue last year was £7,074,000, and the rate per head was £1 15s. 1d.—the highest yet.

Contrast between British and Irish Taxation

But, Sir, the taxation on commodities presses with greater relative as well as absolute severity on Ireland. In Britain, the tax revenue on commodities, which alone affects the masses, in 1820 was, per head, about £2 8s.; in 1894 it was about £1 4s., or half the old rate ; and this kind is now about 53 per cent. of her total taxation. The Irish taxation on commodities in 1820 was, per head, about 11s. ; in 1894 about £1 2s., or double the old rate ; and this comprises 76 per cent. of her total taxation ; and her rate, per head, is now almost equal to that of Great Britain, though the Irish consumption is considerably less.

Contrast in Taxation on Commodities.

The total tax revenue of Ireland is now, including rates,
over eleven millions, while her yearly resources
are, as I conceive, much under seventy millions;
out of which are to be paid, having regard to
the case of the masses—(1) taxation; (2) agricultural rents, including the large economic drain in favour
of absentee landlords and mortgagees; besides the first
charge of all—namely, the subsistence of the masses—say
nearly four and a-half millions of people. This makes
clearly a condition of extraordinary pressure on the means
of subsistence. Taxation must, in bad years, have more than
exhausted the surplus, and so the capital has diminished.
It is, as I have said, near double the maximum relative
capacity. It has now been shown to be beyond the reasonable actual capacity. And the contrast between Ireland and
Britain, with her 1,400 millions of income, is too obvious
to need restatement. That is true which Senior proved
in 1864, that, considering capacity, England is the most
lightly, while Ireland is the most heavily taxed of countries.

Total Irish Taxation: Burden beyond means.

One word on a criticism objecting that this taxation is
not, as my motion asserts, a grievance to all
classes of the Irish community. Sir, setting
aside the feelings which should make it such,
no one who considers the material interests of
the wealthy and their relations to the poor of Ireland can
doubt that they are in the most substantial way damnified
by this excessive burden on the poor, and that redress will
help not one class only but all classes.

Irish Taxation a general grievance.

Now, the second great purpose to which the new
Commission is directed, though the language is condensed and oblique, is to dispute
the possibility of undue burdens through this
indirect taxation. The First Lord of the
Treasury, dealing with this subject on the
eve of the meeting of Parliament, insisted
that if the view of the Commission as to undue burdens
being imposed under indirect taxation of this sort was

Second purpose of New Commission to allege Indirect Taxation no grievance,

sound as between countries, it must be sound as between
individuals, and because it has not been adopted as
between individuals, it is, therefore, not good as between
countries.

But, in establishing your plan for taxing one common
political or geographical area, possessing those

Indirect Taxation in a single country. elements of likeness in economic condition
which render possible or tolerable a common
plan, without exceptions, you are yet obliged
to acknowledge inevitable inequalities in its operation on
individuals, which you minimise so far as you can by your
system, and bear the rest as you must.

Here the case wholly differs. You are dealing with two
countries, which your political Union did not

Case here of two wholly different countries. physically unite or economically assimilate ;
two countries so different that when the Treaty
was made provisions were included for continued separate consideration ; two countries so different
that even in other vital matters their laws remain divergent.
Again, such a consideration of taxation is, of course, much
easier between two countries, the inhabitants being dealt
with as one community, than it would be between each
unit of millions of individuals.

The system may and does press also on the very poor in
Britain. Remedy it for the individual every-

System hard on poor every-where. General remedies. where if you please. Remedy it if you can,
and as far as you can, by changes in the
general system of taxation. Any general
remedy you may apply will so far help to
meet the Irish grievance.

But, in so far as you do not apply an efficient general
remedy you cannot expect Ireland, on which

But Ireland has separate conditions and rights. as a country in consequence of her different
economic conditions, and of the much larger
numbers and narrower means of her very poor,
the grievance presses with much greater weight, to accept
your answer that there is some inequality in Britain too.

The right of separate treatment is recognised by the Treaty. This argument therefore is one against the Treaty. But we are holding by the Treaty, and surely Unionists ought not to depart from it. Unhappily the two countries have more and more diverged in matters relevant to taxation ; and they exist with differing and increasingly different taxable capacities and economic conditions. As the English Commissioners have found :—

" The system of taxation which now exists in the United Kingdom, while it may not be unsuited to the requirements of a rich nation like Great Britain, presses hardly and inequitably on a relatively poorer country like Ireland. Where there is comparatively but little wealth, as in Ireland, the main burden of taxation must of necessity be borne by the consumers of dutiable commodities. The amount thus levied appears to be in excess of what is required by the legitimate needs of Ireland and heavier than the masses of the Irish people ought to be called upon to bear."

These things being so, Ireland has her Treaty right to have the circumstances recognised and weighed in settling her burdens. After all, but an approximation can be reached ; an approximation between the two countries, leaving some inevitable discrepancies as between the individual inhabitants of those countries. But these defects will not justify a refusal to do what is possible, or an attempt to keep an undue burden on Ireland's shoulders.

The First Lord thinks, and the proposed Commission is in part designed to establish, that the indirect

Mr. Balfour's arguments on free will.

character of the taxation deprives Ireland of any right to complain or to separate consideration. But the main or only Irish taxes existing at the Union were indirect, and still quota and exemptions were provided. He complains that the Commissioners in determining the over-taxation of two and three-quarter millions proceeded "by the simple method of argument," and he says the very simplicity of the argument should have created suspicion, for great financial questions are not usually or easily settled by such plain methods. And he objects to "logic and arithmetic" as factors in the case. But he himself resorts to still more simple arguments. He says our views do not apply at all to indirect taxation, because, forsooth,

> "There is an element of free will in the matter. A man may consume or not consume as he pleases. If he does not consume he does not pay. It is surely folly to treat a case of that kind as you would treat a case in which the tax-collector came and took so much money out of his pocket whether he liked it or not."

Now, this in effect is saying that mere consumption, being practically voluntary, is the best test of capacity, for no wrong is done because there is no compulsion to consume. But, Sir, the compulsion comes in when, wanting to consume, craving to consume, needing to consume, you are obliged to pay the State for the power to consume. If this argument were correct, why any provision for exemptions, abatements, or quota? It would be enough to provide that taxation should not be differential, and then indirect taxation would take care of itself; and, since all Irish taxation was then indirect, there would be nothing to take care of. But who would justify now a levelling up in 1800; and who justifies now the levelling up in the years 1853-1860? Yet this argument is ample justification for both. If it were correct, why were the duties kept relatively lower for nearly forty years after the consolidation of the Exchequers? This is, indeed, too "simple" an argument; but I admit it does not sin by the addition of "logic."

The views of the English Commissioners are thus stated:—

> "It has, however, been argued that the articles are, if not luxuries, at any rate superfluities, and therefore fair tests of the balance remaining after the bare necessities of life have been supplied. We are unable to assent to this argument. We think that the consumption of the masses must be taken as a whole, and that we must accept what they actually consume as what they find it necessary to consume, and what, without a total and almost inconceivable change in their habits, they are unable to forego."

The same view is thus expanded in the report of Mr. Sexton:—

> "While equal taxes on property abstract the same proportion only of the income taxed in either country, equal taxes on articles of common consumption operate without any regard to disparity of in-

come. In proportion to the actual consumption of articles of ordinary use, the poorest country, under such a common system, has to pay as much as the richest, at least to the extent to which the taxed articles are consumed in proportion to population. Thus, the poorer country surrenders a larger proportion of gross income, and a still higher proportion of surplus income, even if the rates of consumption of the taxed articles are alike in each. Certain commodities, though taxed, may be consumed in a poorer country almost as much as in a rich one, because the rich has a choice of various articles, while the poor is practically limited to two or three staples on which the tax is laid. The consumption of staples naturally tends to equality, the test being the satisfaction of appetite, so far as the power to acquire exists, and appetites not varying with incomes."

Thus, a tax on articles of very general consumption approximates to a poll-tax. In truth, Sir, it is difficult to treat this argument seriously. On what calculation do you lay such heavy taxes on tobacco, spirits, beer, and tea? Why have you ventured to make these the only contribution of the masses to the public expenditure? How do you dare to count, year after year, on the population paying such sums as—for tea, nineteen and a-half millions; tobacco, twenty-five millions; spirits, fifty-four and three-quarter millions; beer, ninety-five millions— total, one hundred and ninety-four and a-quarter millions —sixty millions more than the value of all your imported foods!—one hundred and ninety-four and a-quarter millions, out of which you derive a "voluntary revenue" of forty-one and a-half millions, on which you depend to pay the greater part of the yearly charge of this empire? The rich you force to pay ; the poor and the masses you do not! They pay only voluntarily, as a matter of free-will! Will this argument satisfy the Englishman when you propose to increase the beer-tax? No ; he will say, " I must have my beer," and he will put out the politician who would "rob a poor man of his beer!" No, Sir ; no! The Chancellor of the Exchequer does not feel on this head much doubt or anxiety. Well, he knows that practically the settled and rooted habits of the people ; their tastes, wants, cravings ; their determination to have and use their tobacco, tea, or liquor ; their need of these articles, are so strong that they

The Truth about Indirect Taxation.

almost amount to *must;* and that it is, in any practical
sense, a mockery to call the tax voluntary. Calmly he
builds his whole financial fabric on the certainty that the
people must have, and, therefore, must pay. He goes gaily
on his way, nor dreads any sudden outbreak of "free-will"
which shall seriously cut down his revenue.

It is said, Sir, that it is the whiskey-tax of which we

*Irish
Complaint.*
complain. There is a serious grievance of
inequality to which I shall have to refer. But,
apart from that, our complaint is of the excessive taxes which are on more than whiskey—which are on
tea, tobacco, and beer as well. You will see by the evidence
as to the poorest districts—for example, Donegal—by the
poor little family budgets which have been presented, so
affecting in the narrowness and bareness of the lives they
depict, that but little whiskey is drunk there ; tea and
tobacco are the only relief.

Then it is said that the whiskey-tax is a tax on excess—

*Whiskey-tax :
Mr.
Courtney's
argument.*
on the drunkard. The right hon. member
for Bodmin used the same argument, saying
that if too much money comes from Ireland
it is because too much whiskey is drunk there,
and that we must fix our attention on the individual who
pays the penalty of the indulgence of his taste ; and he
added that if he suffered a wrong, the wrong would be
doubled if the money were returned to his neighbour. The
First Lord takes a similar line of consideration of the
individual case.

To this whole line of reasoning I demur. The revenue

*Tax general
on sober
masses.*
mainly comes—the efficiency, the productive-
ness of the tax depends upon its coming—from
the masses, who generally take tea, tobacco,
and liquor. The vast proportion of the consumption of liquor is that of the great majority who
are not drunkards. That is the virtue of the tax as a
productive tax. The wideness of the area of pressure
is its strength as a fiscal device. The tax is mainly on

normal, not on excessive consumption. This it is which makes it a general tax—a tax on the masses; and so an object of substantial justice would be achieved, if abatement or exemption were impossible, by remission or restitution to the masses of the community. It were truly a refinement of justice for Britain to refuse any remedy, any relief, for fear that the restoration to the Irish community of excessive taxation on individuals composing the Irish masses shall not exactly apportion the return to the individual taxpayer. Is this the reason why there is to be no redress? It would be a shabby excuse, which I hardly expected to hear urged in this place; but which I suspect is intended from one of the proposed references to the new Commission.

But, Sir, the accusation of comparative excess which underlies this argument I dispute, and challenge the accusers. I wish there were less drinking in Ireland and in Britain. But Ireland, compared with Britain, is a sober country. You who accuse us spend far more on drink than we; and you arrange to get it cheap, at Irish and Scottish expense. You are provident in your cups. There is here a gross inequality under a nominally equal system. It is not necessary to go to hypothetical cases, as of tea-drinking and coffee-drinking countries united for taxation. Let us take the case of the beer and the whiskey-drinking countries. Not merely is the whole sum of Irish taxation relatively excessive, but the spirit and the beer taxes are also, as between themselves, grossly unequal and partial in their operation.

Charge of Irish excess untrue.

Let us look at the facts. I take Britain as a whole Scotland has a case here against England even more aggravated than ours; and to strike the account with Britain as a whole thus lessens unduly the Irish claim as against England. But the reference is as between Great Britain and Ireland.

Comparative Drink Bills— Britain and Ireland.

In 1893 the expenditure for beer in Britain was

Beer. £88,627,000, or £2 13s. a head ; in Ireland, £6,291,000, or £1 7s. 2d. a head. Thus the Briton spends all but twice as much on beer as the Irishman. "Oh," you may say, "we all know that! The Briton drinks beer, the Irishman whiskey ; what about whiskey ? "

Well, Sir, what about whiskey? The expenditure for

Whiskey. spirits in Britain was £48,571,000, or £1 9s. per head ; in Ireland, £6,144,000, or £1 6s. 6d. per head. Thus, much more was spent per head on spirits in Britain than in Ireland. So Britain preserved her superiority in both branches of this competition ; having spent twice as much on beer, she took a good deal more spirits, too ; and then she says something about Irish drunkards ! The Briton spends on both £4 2s. ; the Irishman, £2 13s. 8d. And then some British statesman tells his enthusiastic constituents that the Irish complaint is due to too much drink ; and if they would only purge and live cleanly they would have no ground for grievance. I venture to suggest that it is not for Britain to "cast a stone," to preach free-will, temperance, and soberness as our cure, or to defend injustice on her part by alleging excess on ours.

But this is not all, or nearly all. As I have said, you are

Unjust Taxation as between Beer and Spirits. provident in your cups. See how you have arranged the cost of that part which you can control—the tax. You prefer beer, and the tax on beer is alike for all. So is the tax on spirits alike for all. But the tax on sixty gallons of your favourite drink—beer—is equal to the tax on one gallon of whiskey. Having regard to the relative quantity of alcohol, the tax on beer is about one-sixth of the tax on spirits. The tax on beer is about one-sixth of the selling price in bulk ; the tax on spirits about three-fourths of the selling price. What is the practical result of these equal taxes? The tax revenue, Imperial and local, was for 1893—in

Britain—Spirits, £13,810,000 ; beer, £9,214,000—a total of £23,024,000. In Ireland—Spirits, £2,240,000 ; beer, £624,000—a total of £2,764,000. The Briton's drink bill was £4 2s., out of which 16s. 1d. was tax ; the Irishman's, £2 13s. 6d., out of which 13s. 10½d. was tax. If the Irishman paid only at the Briton's rate his tax would be 10s. 6d. ; his excess is 3s. 4½d., which for Ireland is no less than seven hundred and eighty thousand pounds a year! I have not run out the figures for Ireland as against England alone, but I fancy the excess would cover eight hundred and fifty thousand pounds a year.

But this, according to the free-will doctrine of the First Lord, is, I must admit, no grievance. The Irishman may differ in taste and in opinion, and difference of climate may affect his judgment as to the kind of drink most suitable for him. But these are mere details. The Briton likes his beer and likes it cheap ; and so the Irishman must have the free will to like it too ; and thus he can save the tax ! Indeed the unequal pressure of the tax has been operating to some extent in this direction.

Mr. Balfour's free will again.

I am not now arguing as to the expediency, in the general interest, of changes in these duties, or of differential rates. You may contend that on moral, or economic, or fiscal grounds it would be a misfortune so to lower the duty on spirits, and a political impossibility so to raise the duty on beer as to produce equality, and a bad thing to have differential duties. But those contentions do not settle the question. If they be true, none the less is there a grievance to Ireland ; none the less should that grievance be met in some other way as a part of the fiscal arrangement ; none the less should the spirit of the compact be observed. You should not promote your morality, or interest, or convenience at our expense. I ask the House, concurring in the finding of the joint Report that "identity of rates of taxation does not necessarily involve equality of burden," to agree also to the

Difficulty of change no excuse.

view, that I have proved, in the case of these two countries, gross inequalities demanding redress.

Well, Mr. Speaker, complaints of excessive taxation have been made for generations from the Irish

Irish com-
plaints and
Parliamentary
enquiries,
1864. benches. In 1864 the House referred it to a Select Committee, "to consider the taxation of Ireland ; how far it is in accordance with the Treaty of Union, or just in reference to the resources of the country," and a long inquiry took place. The Irish contention was then met by adopting the fallacious idea of the taxation of individuals instead of the taxation of the country, and by ignoring the relevant considerations as to the practical effect of taxes on articles of primary use and general consumption.

But, be it remembered, that there was then no suggestion of divided estimates ; those who resisted the

No proposal
to divide
expenditure
then. Irish claim did not found themselves no that construction. They took advantage of the opposite view—the one by which we hold ; and for a very good reason. In the sixties, when Ireland in one year paid £7,700,000, of which, even according to the preposterous divisions now suggested, £5,400,000 went to what is now called Imperial expenditure, the modern argument would have made bad worse ; and according to it there would, during many years have been, as there is, an enormous balance overpaid by Ireland, aggregating many millions. At that time it suited Britain to adopt the other and truer view, namely, that local circumstances and conditions might involve a greater expenditure by the United Kingdom in one than in the other country ; that it was none the less common; due to, growing out of, and material to the Union ; expenditure of the United Kingdom.

There were in later years ineffectual motions and remonstrances. But the question became

Home Rule:
1886. demonstrably urgent on the occasion of the Home Rule Bill of 1886, when the financial proposals involved the re-consideration of the whole problem, coupled with an attempt, in view of Irish self-government, to divide what had been the United Kingdom expenditure into Imperial and local, based, of course, on the respective legislative spheres of the Imperial and the proposed local Legislatures. This event is the clue to much that has since occurred in this connection.

In 1890, when, after the question of Home Rule had been placed before the country, a Unionist Government was in power, the present First Lord of the Admiralty, then Chancellor of the Exchequer, in reply to a request from these benches, said :—

Mr. Goschen's action, 1890; separate entity.

" I think we shall be prepared to grant an inquiry into the financial relations of the two countries. I do not want to exclude Scotland, and I think hon. members from both countries will see that we are anxious to meet them. We shall be glad to throw as much light as possible on the financial relations of the two countries. Hon. members will see at once that it must be a full and proper inquiry. Of course, if the inquiry should show that injustice has been done to any part of the United Kingdom steps will be taken to afford redress."

The right hon. gentleman, after consulting his colleagues later, in making the motion objected to any historical retrospect. The purpose, he said, was—

"To see whether Scotland or Ireland should be relieved of any portion of the taxation they now pay ; to see if there should be any alteration of existing burdens. . . . The power of a country to pay taxation must to a large extent depend on numbers. I trust all these matters will be thrashed out in the Committee."

The Committee sat but once, when it called for Treasury returns. Efforts to re-appoint it failed because of objections taken by the Welsh members, who claimed a similar separate consideration for Wales, which the Government declined to grant on the ground that Wales had never been treated as a separate fiscal entity.

The financial returns which have been presented for several years had here their origin. Now, this proceeding and language involved the recognition of the right of Ireland and Scotland as countries to separate consideration ; and more, the acknowledgment that the indirect system of

The Financial Relations Papers.

taxation did not automatically produce taxation according
to resources ; and that the resources of the countries were
to be considered, the alleged equal operation of the taxation on the individual inhabitants not answering the
demand.   The maintenance of such views would have
cut away the ground for the committee.   It seems to me
obvious that the form of the reference and returns was in
part moulded by the recent attempts to make a division in
connection with the Home Rule scheme.

Again there have been recognitions in recent years of
the separate condition of Ireland and Scotland in connection with the Imperial grants
in aid of local rates.   I refer to, without
implying approval of, the system.   But how
has it been worked ?   These grants were based not on the
plan of applying the total aid all over the United Kingdom,
as one taxable entity, but on the theory (though not without exception later as against Ireland) that each of the
three divisions was a taxable unit to which was being
returned, for expenditure by the minor local authorities, a
portion of the general taxation ; and, therefore, that the
return should be on the basis of the proportions in which
each of the units had contributed to the fund.

Imperial Grants in aid of rates.

Last Session when agricultural distress throughout the
United Kingdom was to be aided this device
was, as many of us think, most unwarrantably
expanded, so as to limit the relief of Ireland—
the country in which there existed the greatest
agricultural distress—by making the grant, in form, a
relief to local rates in England, and thus applying, as we
think erroneously, the proportional system.   And so, those
who oppose our view that we are entitled to separate
treatment as to taxation, themselves insist, in some degree,
on separate treatment in expenditure.

Agricultural Distress Relief, 1896.

Now, Sir, it is acknowledged by Sir Edward Hamilton
that the Union Act does not contemplate this division.
But he says, and others say, that circumstances have

altered since, that some expenditures are now made which
were not then made, as, for example, on
No right to
alter treaty. Police and Education. True, enlarged con-
ceptions have been formed of the duty of the
Government of the United Kingdom; and it has been
deemed to be a national object to provide for the education and for the order of the people; and, for its government under the Union, a constabulary has been organised
in Ireland. Accordingly Acts have been passed and
revenue is raised and expended by the United Kingdom
for this purpose. But this does not in the least alter the
rights of Ireland, or render obsolete the provisions of the
treaty. This is your own interpretation of the duty of the
United Kingdom.

But it is said that a part of the expenditure on education
and on police is, under Imperial legislation,
Argument
from British
rates. provided for in Britain by local rates, raised
by local bodies, who have been given a
measure of control over the subjects, and that
it is unfair to ignore this local expenditure in stating the
account between the countries. I repeat that it is impossible for this reason to divest the expenditure of the
Imperial character which it clearly retains, so far as Ireland
is concerned. You make it and you keep it Imperial; and
its scale, its purpose, its regulation, are all such as you
choose to fix, not such as you are willing to confide to
local representative authorities. We must therefore hold
by the view that the money which this Parliament votes,
expends, and controls, for the purpose of carrying on
government in Ireland is in reason, and in the sense of the
Union Act, Imperial expenditure.

This view is our only protection against the injustice
which would ensue from your being at liberty
Mode of
meeting
objection. to fix the scale and direct the mode, while we
are obliged to pay. And the objection of in-
equality would be fully met, if for the purpose
of ascertaining the grand total to which Ireland should
contribute, the analogous amount raised locally in Britain

towards these two objects were added to the sum of the
Imperial estimate. Thus Ireland would bear her proportionate share of the whole expenditure; and this would
meet in a less objectionable way the position of Mr.
Childer's as to Police and Education, and in very large
measure the criticisms of Lord Farrer and his colleagues.
This, I need hardly say, is a very narrow question. The
data are accessible; the figures can be easily run out.
There are some minor cross-entries to be made. The
general result would be perhaps so to enlarge the total
Imperial estimate as to reduce the over-taxation by about
£300,000, or to about two and a half millions on the
minimum estimate. I need hardly say that the adoption
of this plan, with its limited and defined application, affords
not the least justification for the proposed breaking up of
the Imperial expenditure, which it rather keeps intact;
still less does it need a new Royal Commission.

But it is said our contention would make Britain
tributary to Ireland. Not so; every detail
of the whole affair is within your power, and
is moulded according to your will.

Then, if for argument's sake, the principle of breaking
up the Imperial expenditure be admitted, we
quarrel grievously with the details. On these
also all the data for judgment are before us,
and the questions are peculiarly for settle-
ment by Parliament on the initiative of the
Government. As Lord Farrer said in another place, they
need no new Commission. The speech of the First Lord
adopted the classification of the Treasury, and based on
it the assertion that Ireland contributed but 1-32nd to
what he called Imperial expenditure. Now, let me glance
at the details of this division.

Ireland is charged with the Constabulary—an armed,
semi-military force, maintained at enormous
cost, far beyond any conceivable need for the
policing, under normal conditions, of such a country; a
force and a scale of expenditure directly flowing from and

due to the Union, and doing almost entirely Imperial work. I do not find that any one of the Commissioners, or even Sir Edward Hamilton himself, approves this charge in its totality, and he states that in the earliest of the Financial Relations Papers it was distributed as Imperial. So it ought to be.

Ireland is charged with the Imperial expenditure on the great national subject of education, which is Education. moulded and directed through Imperial legislation, by Imperial and centralised administration.

Ireland is charged with the collection of the Imperial revenue, the administration of justice, the Other charges. Post Office, the Civil Service generally, the Viceregal establishment. All these are obviously Imperial.

Then we quarrel with the scale of expenditure, created here and proposed to be charged exclusively Scale of to us. It is expensive, extravagant, centra-Expenditure. lized, on the Imperial scale. Look at the salaries and numbers of the judges, and contrast the conditions as between the emoluments of Bar and Bench, even with these which prevail here, still more with those which prevail in poorer countries. Contrast the cost of departments compared with the cost even here. The whole system is unsuited to the circumstances and beyond the means of Ireland. It is not checked by the ordinary safeguards of local responsibility and the ordinary inducements to economy. All these are defects in the system. From it they flow. With what justice then do you propose to charge them exclusively on the weaker partner?

But you say, "Irishmen and Irish members will not cut down the votes." After all, it is you who frame Irish part in the estimates and pass the votes. But give to extravagance. Ireland the usual stimulus to economy—some profit from the saving, before you complain that she does not insist on pruning your extravagance. While she finds that she is taxed beyond her capacity; that she will not appreciably gain by economy in Ireland; and that the only

question is where the money shall be spent, is it much
wonder that she should prefer Ireland as the scene?
At any rate the responsibility is yours ; Ireland cannot save
or spend a shilling ; you have the power and must take
the blame.

But, Sir, it is not only to the Irish part of this divided
estimate that we object. We object to the
Imperial part as well. If you cut up the estimates as you propose, and find some elements
to which, as Imperial, you hold us specially
bound to make proportionate contribution, you drive us to
analyse their nature, and to inquire whether there is any
reasonable ground for our providing, first, everything you
choose to call local expenditure, and then also our proportion, according to our relative taxable capacity, of these
great heads of Imperial expenditure.

Objection to proposed Imperial contribution.

I do not, in the present form of Union, want to open any
of these questions. I believe they cannot be
opened without violating the spirit of the Act.
I believe the Act contemplates and provides
that Ireland should contribute towards the expenditure of
the Imperial Parliament, no matter where that money be
spent or how it be applied, whether here, or in Ireland, or
abroad, according to her relative taxable capacity.

True view. No division.

But if you will destroy this system, cut up the accounts,
and enter into the question of the separate or
relative interests of Britain and of Ireland in
the different expenditures, depend upon it you
will have to grapple with your Imperial as
well as with your local estimates. We rest on the contract ;
you propose a change. Then must we look at the new
Imperial estimates.

But, if change, then inquiry.

Look at your navy. Britain has created an economic
system under which she requires, in order that
she may obtain her supplies of food and of
materials, and maintain her position as a
manufacturing, mercantile, and carrying power, to keep

Imperial Navy.

command of the sea. Her naval budget is her insurance premium. She is continually pressed to add to her insurance, and told that it is cheap. It may be cheap for her; she has the gains. But can you honestly say that Ireland has the same proportionate interest in the profits insured by this premium? And, if not, can you say she ought to contribute in that proportion to the insurance?

Look at your army, mainly required for the purposes of the Indian and Colonial Empire, and for the security of your commercial interests, and to which therefore the same considerations apply. Look at your debt charge, contracted for wars waged in the same interests.

Imperial Army.

Imperial Debt.

Do not charge me with taking a limited or a shopkeeper's view of this matter. Remember the language of the Prime Minister and Foreign Secretary, uttered as late as the 11th March, when he said—

Lord Salisbury's views.

"All machinery—at all events of the external part of our Government—is in its intention and its object directed for the purpose of maintaining and facilitating British trade. We have heard and we rejoice at the great achievements of our army and our navy—how they have never failed us under any stress to which they have been put. But the object of all this action is that the various parts of the world may be kept open to the exploration, to the enterprise, to the industry of Britain, may be saved from that encircling band of hostile tariffs which causes us to know, when we hear that a territory has fallen into foreign occupation, that it is really robbed from British trade."

Sir, I think these considerations show that the proposed inquiry would, if it ever ended, never satisfy, and that the only safe ground is to stand on the Union Act provisions. Let me repeat, I do not wish to open these matters. It is you, who set up this suggested division of expenditure, who raise the issue. But while I thus contend, I fully agree that, if this whole question were taken up by Britain in the proper spirit, it would become our duty and our interest to promote all reasonable reductions in the extravagance of Irish expenditure.

General result.

There remains only one set off on which I wish to say a single word. I refer to the remitted or unsettled advances or grants to Ireland. With part I have already dealt—namely, the famine advances. Of the remainder, some are being settled by the Restitution Fund. Of the bulk it is to be remarked that they were not at all advances to local authorities, or analogous to the British grants, but expenditures made by the Imperial Government, largely wasteful and futile, and charged compulsorily on the people. The sum total seems in fairness reducible to about one million in excess of remissions of English advances; but if it all stood, it would form only a fraction of the restitution fairly due to Ireland in respect of past over-taxation, an element of the grievance which demands redress. On this, too, all the materials are before us, and the question is ripe for your decision.

Loans and advances.

Now, Sir, an amendment has been put down insisting on the absolute fiscal indivisibility of the United Kingdom, and on the consideration only of the pressure of taxation on the individual, wherever he may reside. This was partly the view of the Committee of 1864. But it is not, as I think I have shown, the true view.

Mr. Whittaker's amendment.

Another amendment appears, designed at once seriously to limit the range and to indicate one direction of remedial legislation. But I venture to submit to my right hon. friend that it is both a wiser course and a truer interpretation of Irish opinion to adhere to the comprehensive words of my proposal.

Mr. Plunkett's amendment.

The line of the Government is different. It does not in terms adopt, though it may aim at the result of, the first amendment. It does not acknowledge the existence of a grievance, or admit the propriety of the remedy suggested by the second amendment. The Government proposes to meet

The Government line.

the case by the appointment of a new Commission, mainly
to inquire into the results of the proposed division into four
parts of the United Kingdom expenditure, into the effect
of the existing United Kingdom taxation, and into the
propriety of changes in taxation and expenditure. In a
word, it is proposed to deal with our demand upon the
lines of the speech of the First Lord of the Treasury at
Manchester. I have already given you the reasons why I
think it impossible to assent to any such inquiry.

It is said that the Commissioners failed to discharge
their duty by not reporting upon this question
of division. But the bulk of the Commissioners held that that portion of the reference
had regard to the political conditions then
existing as to Home Rule, and had no foundation under
the Act of Union. That is the argument we advance.

*The
Commis-
sioners' view.*

This, however, is to be added, that all the materials for
a conclusion upon these questions have been
collected, and are to be found in the proceedings of the Commission ; and that there
is no necessity or utility in remitting
such questions at this day to the decision of any such body.
They are now, after all, peculiarly a matter for Parliament.
Upon the ground then, first, that the proposed inquiry is
based upon wrong principles ; secondly, that it is useless ;
and thirdly, that it is dilatory, we object to and protest
against the Commission.

*New
Commission
useless.*

This being the answer to our demand, I am relieved
from considering in detail the suggestion
which has been thrown out in Ministerial
quarters, that the Commission should have
indicated, and that we, forsooth, should now
indicate the precise form of the remedy. That question
was not referred to the Commission. It is obviously one
for Parliament, on the initiative of the Executive, to deal
with. It is not for us, a small minority, powerless to
achieve, to propound the specific remedy to-day.

*Demand for
specific
remedy.*

You well know what the majority of the Irish people
think would embrace a complete and effective

Home Rule.   remedy.   That solution you refuse to adopt.

But your refusal entails on you even added responsi-
bilities towards Ireland ; and, both as the

Responsibility   depositories of power and as the special de-
of Unionist
Party.   fenders of the existing form of Union, which
is the basis of this Government, you are
doubly bound to find a remedy for this grievous injustice,
existent under the system you maintain and control.

Several plans have been suggested, of which some are
to be found in the various reports.   All may

Several plans   have their inconveniences.   It is for you to
in reports.
propound that which you think best, and for
us to make counter-proposals.   But, the principle of our
claim once admitted, we shall make no difficulty in discuss-
ing with you the best remedy.

If you say " The inconveniences are too serious ; we find
no practicable way within the Union ; there-

Consequences   fore the grievance must remain unredressed,"
of refusal.
then assuredly, the friends of the Union will
inflict a heavy blow on the system by which they stand.   You
have declared for that Union as a compact under which
Ireland was secure in all her rights, and protected in all her
interests ; under which she was assured of just and generous
treatment.   If you now aver that the Union demands that
she shall still labour under this injustice, you cannot but
discourage its friends, and place in the hands of its op-
ponents a keen and powerful weapon of attack.

Sir, we call for *action*, and to that end I move—" That
in the opinion of this house the report and proceedings of
the Royal Commission on the Financial Relations of Great
Britain and Ireland establish the existence of an undue
burden of taxation on Ireland, which constitutes a great
grievance to all classes of the Irish community, and makes it
the duty of the Government to propose at an early day
remedial legislation."

Tables

Arranged, with assistance, by the Editor.

———◆———

The References are principally to the *Report* and Two Volumes of *Evidence*
of the Financial Relations Commission.

Parl. Papers, C. 8262, 1896, and C. 7720, I. II. 1895.

———◆———

FRACTIONS UNDER 1000 HAVE IN MOST CASES BEEN OMITTED.

Tables.

I.

POPULATION OF GREAT BRITAIN AND IRELAND FROM 1780 TO 1896.

[The figures for Great Britain are taken principally from Census Reports; those for Ireland from Dr. Grimshaw's Tables, *Evidence*, II. 437-8. Those for 1896 are from Registrar-Generals' Estimates.]

Year.	Great Britain.	Ireland.
1780	9,510,000	3,526,000
1791	10,055,000	4,206,000
1801	10,942,000	4,937,000
1811	12,596,000	5,795,000
1821	14,329,000	6,802,000
1831	16,260,000	7,767,000
1841	18,534,000	8,199,000
1851	20,815,000	6,514,000
1861	23,128,000	5,788,000
1871	26,072,000	5,398,000
1881	29,709,000	5,145,000
1891	33,027,000	4,681,000
1896	34,917,000	4,560,000

II.

EXPENDITURE PER HEAD OF POPULATION ON SPIRITS AND BEER IN GREAT BRITAIN AND IN IRELAND IN 1893.

[Parl. Paper 334 of 1893, *Evidence*, I. 360.]

—	Great Britain.	Ireland.
Spirits	£1 9 0	£1 6 6
Beer	2 13 0	1 7 2
Totals ...	£4 2 0	£2 13 8

III.

Tax Revenue of Great Britain and of Ireland from 1782-3 to 1893-4, According to the Treasury Tables of Net Revenue, from 1782-3 to 1800-1, inclusive ; of Total Revenue from 1801-2 to 1816-7, inclusive ; and of Estimated True Revenue from 1819-20 to 1893-4.

[See Tables put in *Evidence* by Sir E. W. Hamilton, Assistant-Secretary to the Treasury, I. 368-9, 371-2, and II. 191.]

[Also, note :—Up to 1801 for Great Britain, and to 1821 for Ireland, the population is estimated. From 1801 (inclusive) for Great Britain, and 1821 (inclusive) for Ireland, the Census figures are taken.]

		Great Britain.			Ireland.	
		Tax Revenue.	Per head.		Per head.	Tax Revenue.
		£	£ s. d.		£	£ s. d.
	1782-83 ...	11,880,000	1 5 0	Estimated.	814,000	0 4 0
	1792-93 ...	16,519,000	1 12 0		1,016,000	0 4 0
	1801-02 ...	33,596,000	3 4 0		2,521,000	0 10 0
	1809-10 ...	61,275,000	5 2 0		4,687,000	0 16 0
The amounts per head, as well as the totals of Revenue, for 1819-20, and thenceforward, to 1893-94, are extracted from Sir E. W. Hamilton's Table, II. p. 191.	1819-20 ...	49,511,000	3 10 3		4,911,000	0 14 5
	1829-30 ...	47,416,000	2 18 0		5,067,000	0 13 1
	1839-40 ...	43,918,000	2 7 5		5,076,000	0 12 5
	1849-50 ...	49,651,000	2 7 8		4,563,000	0 13 11
	1859-60 ...	57,866,000	2 10 0		7,340,000	1 5 4
	1869-70 ...	59,678,000	2 5 9		6,868,000	1 5 5
	1879-80 ...	60,060,000	2 0 5		6,437,000	1 4 11
	1889-90 ...	71,588,000	2 3 4		6,820,000	1 9 0
	1893-94 ...	75,796,000	2 4 10		6,643,000	*1 8 10

* Increased in 1895-6 to £1 15s. 1d.

Statistics such as are here given form the basis of Ireland's contention regarding over-taxation. Since 1809-10, the taxation of Great Britain has been reduced from £5 2s. to £2 4s. 10d. per head ; that of Ireland has been increased from 16s. to £1 15s. 1d. per head. The proportions of taxation have not been adhered to, against which even the Irish Lords recorded their protest, and by which a bare majority of the Irish Commons were induced to agree to the Union,

IV.

PRINCIPAL PAYMENTS FROM IRELAND TO ENGLAND CONSTITUTING A
DRAIN ON THE ECONOMIC RESOURCES OF IRELAND, *i.e.*, PAY-
MENTS AND EXPENDITURE OUT OF THE ANNUAL GROSS INCOME OF
IRELAND FOR WHICH THERE IS LITTLE OR NO CORRESPONDING
RETURN.

[Mr. Murrough O'Brien's Table, *Evidence* II. 196.]

—	Amount known approximately.	Probable Amount.
	£	£
1. Value of property owned by absentees, confined to rural property as per Return 167 of April 23, 1872.*	2,470,816	⎫
2. Similar proportion of Urban properties ...	960,900	⎬ 5,000,000
3. Residue of London Co.'s estates	30,000	⎭
4. Mortgages of English Insurance Co.'s as estimated by Dr. Giffen in 1886, £14,000,000 at 4½ per cent.†	630,000	1,500,000 (all absentee mortgages and annuities)
5. Average amount paid by Church Fund as interest for 23 years to 31st March, 1894	219,631	219,631
6. Average annual amount of capital repaid by Church Fund for 19 years.	379,769	379,769
7. Interest on Board of Works and Public Works Loan Commissioners Loans average taken as payment in 1893. (Smith-Barry's Return 376, 17th August, 1893.) ‡	265,137	265,137
8. Repayment of capital by same return ...	430,686	430,686
9. Quit-rents and Crown Reversions ...	40,000	40,000
10. Land Loan Annuities 4 per cent. on £12,000,000.	480,000	480,000
11. Remittances of capital for deposit in Post Office and Trustee Savings Banks. Average annual increase of deposits for past 21 half years.	254,760	254,760
12. Interest at 1 per cent. on Post Office and Trustee Bank deposits on which 2½ per cent. is paid to depositors, while they are lent back to Ireland at not less than 3½ per cent.	65,000	65,000
13. Extra cost of Irish Private Bill legislation, estimated (*see* debate in 1871) to cost for witnesses five times as much as if conducted in Ireland.	Not ascertained.	—
14. Expenses of 100 M.P.'s at £300 each per session.	30,000	30,000
	£6,256,699	£8,664,983

* This return was well known to be an under estimate; superior rents, rentcharges, and annuities were not included in it. Absenteeism has increased since 1872.
† The mortgage debt on Irish real estate has been estimated at from 80 to 120 millions by authorities. Irish mortgages were for many years a favourite investment for English lenders owing to the higher rate of interest obtainable.
‡ The benefit of most of this expenditure is represented in the assessment returns and rental.

V.

TAXABLE CAPACITY OF IRELAND, AS COMPARED TO THAT OF GREAT BRITAIN.

[Calculated: Nos. 1 to 8, 15 and 16, from Sir Robert Giffen's Tables, *Evidence*, II. 173. No. 9 from Mr. Murrough O'Brien's Table, *Evidence*, I. 387. Nos. 10 to 13 from Sir E. W. Hamilton's Table, *Evidence*, I. 356-7. No. 14. See Table VI.]

	In Ireland compared with that in Great Britain is as		
1. Consumption of Coal	1	to	41
2. Nett Income Tax Assessments of Quarries, Mines and Gasworks	1	,,	58
3. Tonnage of Shipping in Foreign Trade ...	1	,,	58
4. Persons engaged in Textile Factories ...	1	,,	62
5. Capital of Joint Stock Companies ...	1	,,	43
6. Passengers (exclusive of Season Ticket Holders) carried on Railways	1	,,	36
7. Goods conveyed on Railways	1	,,	71
8. Value of Mineral Produce	1	,,	416
9. Capital of Industrial and Provident Societies	1	,,	832
10. Income from Government Stocks (average of years 1891, 1892, 1893)	1	,,	53 ·
11. Profits derived from Trades and Professions (same period)	1	,,	32
12. Total Profits assessed to Income-Tax (same period)	1	,,	21
13. Property assessed to Probate and Succession Duty (same period)	1	,,	20
14. Surplus Income after deducting cost of Subsistence and Taxation	1	,,	27

	Ireland.	Great Britain.
15. Males above 20 in Agricultural Class in 1891	701,000	1,146,000
16. Nett Agricultural Production	£40,000,000	£180,000,000
Average per person	£57	£157

It is upon figures such as these that Ireland's low taxable capacity, as compared to Great Britain, is established. The two last lines prove that even in her one great industry, agriculture, her people are at a disadvantage.

VI.

APPROXIMATE CAPITAL OF GREAT BRITAIN AND OF IRELAND IN 1895, WITH APPROXIMATE ESTIMATE OF SURPLUS INCOME OF INHABITANTS IN BOTH COUNTRIES.

[Evidence *passim*, and Mr. Murrough O'Brien's Table, *Evidence*, I. 388.]

	Great Britain.	Ireland.
	£	£
Capital in 1812	1,500,000,000	563,000,000
„ 1895	10,000,000,000	400,000,000
Gross Annual Income, 1895	1,500,000,000	70,000,000
Maintenance Allowance, £12 per head of population	420,000,000	55,000,000
	1,080,000,000	15,000,000
Revenue, 1892-93 ... Great Britain 88,000,000 Ireland 7,000,000		
Local Taxes ... 39,000,000 3,000,000	127,000,000	10,000,000
Surplus above bare Maintenance	953,000,000* about £27 per head	5,000,000 about £1 per head

* More according to some Evidence.

VII.

THE EXTENT TO WHICH IN IRELAND, AS COMPARED TO IN GREAT BRITAIN, TAXES ARE RAISED OFF COMMODITIES IN GENERAL USE BY THE PEOPLE.

[From Sir Edward W. Hamilton's Tables, *Evidence* II. 192.]

Years.	Great Britain. Indirect Taxes on Commodities, etc. Per cent.	Direct and other Taxes. Per cent.	Ireland. Indirect Taxes on Commodities, etc. Per cent.	Direct and other Taxes. Per cent.
1819-1820	69·1	30·9	76·4	23·6
1829-1830	72·6	27·4	87·9	12·1
1839-1840	72·4	27·6	89·2	10·8
1849-1850	63·4	36·6	87·3	12·7
1859-1860	63·2	36·8	81·3	18·7
1869-1870	56·0	44·0	80·7	19·3
1879-1880	58·2	41·8	80·6	19·4
1889-1890	53·5	46·5	80·0	20·0
1893-1894	53·7	46·3	76·4	23·6

VIII.

PROPORTIONS OF MARRIAGES, BIRTHS, AND DEATHS IN THE THREE KINGDOMS.

Per 1,000 of Population, average-1871–92. [Registrar-General, *Evidence* I. 390.]	England.	Scotland.	Ireland.
Persons who Married	15·6	13·9	9·0
Births	34·0	33·6	24·9
Deaths	20·3	20·4	18·0
Excess of Births over Deaths [Sir Robert Giffen's Table, *Evidence* II. 162.] Per 1,000 of Population	11·5	11·4	5·0
Estimated Average Marrying Age. [Mulhall's *Statistics*, 1892.] Males	27·7	28·6	29·9
Females	25·5	25·7	25·2

Upon the figures, such as these, Sir Robert Giffen remarks (*Evidence*, II. 162-3):—" What is found by experience to be a most significant sign of general economic conditions is the . . . excess of births over deaths. A high excess, when combined, as it usually is, with a low death rate, and with a moderate if not a low birth rate, is a good sign of prosperity. . . . Ireland has more people in proportion above 50 than Great Britain has, and fewer people in prime of life, *i.e.*, between 20 and 40. The difference is sensible. In Ireland no less than 18·6 per cent. of the male population are upwards of 50, but in Scotland and England the per-centages are 13·5 and 13·7 respectively. The per-centage in Ireland between 20 and 40 is 26·6 per cent., and in Scotland and England 28·9 and 29·9 respectively. The per-centages of the female population are much the same. Ireland has thus fewer people in proportion in the prime of life and more above 50 than Great Britain has. . . . These figures also agree with the facts as to the composition of emigration from Ireland and Great Britain respectively. In Ireland there is a steadier stream of people in the prime of life."

IX.

EMIGRATION FROM ENGLAND, SCOTLAND AND IRELAND, 1880 TO 1894.
[Calculated from Sir Robert Giffen's Table, *Evidence* II. 175.]

—	England.	Scotland.	Ireland.
Male Emigrants	1,155,000	189,000	460,000
Female ,, ...	634,000	112,000	430,000
Children ,, ...	376,000	78,000	123,000
Proportion of Males to Females ...	100 to 55	100 to 59	100 to 93
Proportion of Children in Total ...	17 per cent.	20 per cent.	12 per cent.

This striking Table suggests the extent to which Irish emigration is drawn from the presumably young, unmarried portion of the population in the prime of life, and the degree in which thereby the country is depleted of the life-giving portion of its population.

X.

REVENUE FROM TEA, COCOA, CHICORY AND COFFEE, AND TOBACCO
CONTRIBUTED BY GREAT BRITAIN AND BY IRELAND, 1893-4.

[As computed by Treasury (Paper C 313, of 1894) *Evidence*, I. 408.]

—	Great Britain.	Ireland.	Irish as to British Contribution.
	£	£	
Tea	3,004,000	489,000	I to 6⅛
Cocoa ...	90,000	12,000	I ,, 7⅝
Coffee and Chicory ...	210,000	12,000	I ,, 17⅜
Tobacco	8,945,000	1,174,000	I ,, 7⅝
	12,249,000	1,687,000	I ,, 7¼

Compare these figures with the taxable capacity, "not estimated by any
of" the eleven Commissioners "as exceeding one-twentieth."

XI.

AVERAGE ANNUAL VALUE OF CROPS AND STOCK IN IRELAND, FOUR
PERIODS BETWEEN 1851-55 AND 1889-93.

[Dr. Grimshaw's Tables, *Evidence*, I. 451-3.]

—	Crops.	Stock.	Total.
	£	£	£
1851-55	58,537,000	39,348,000	97,885,000
1866-70	45,365,000	59,630,000	104,995,000
1884-88	35,752,000	55,827,000	91,579,000
1889-93	34,643,000	54,312,000	88,955,000

AVERAGE ANNUAL VALUE DISPOSED OF, EXCLUSIVE OF THE PORTION
OF CROPS USED BY STOCK.

—	Crops.	Stock.	Total.
	£	£	£
1851-55	43,663,000	28,325,000	71,988,000
1866-70	27,935,000	44,279,000	72,214,000
1884-88	16,466,000	37,548,000	54,014,000
1889-93	Not given.	—	—

XII.

TABLE SHOWING THE INCREASE OF PAUPERISM IN IRELAND WITHIN
PAST THIRTY YEARS.

[Mr. H. A. Robinson's Table, *Evidence*, II. 198.]

YEAR.	In Workhouses and Institutions for the Blind, etc.	In receipt of Outdoor Relief (approximately).	Total daily average number.	Percentage of Total daily average on population.
	Average daily number in receipt of relief.			
1862-3	58,301	6,263	64,564	1·12
1867-8	54,195	14,940	69,135	1·26
1872-3	47,325	27,509	74,834	1·40
1877-8	47,749	33,547	81,296	1·53
1882-3	51,097	58,835	109,932	2·19
1887-8	46,105	65,506	111,611	2·31
1892-3	41,549	59,137	100,686	2·17

XIII.

PROPORTION OF BLIND, DEAF AND DUMB, AND INSANE PERSONS IN
GREAT BRITAIN AND IN IRELAND, IN 1891.

[English Census, 1891, *Evidence*, II. 209-210.]

	Number per Million.		
	England and Wales.	Scotland.	Ireland.
Blind	809	695	1,135
Deaf and Dumb	489	528	715
Insane	3,358	3,841	4,504

Here is shown the inevitable outcome of drain upon resources and the
emigration of the young and vigorous.

PUBLICATIONS RELATING TO THE OVER-TAXATION OF IRELAND.

———◆———

In addition to numerous articles in Magazines and separate publications, such as the reports of speeches by Sir EDWARD CLARKE and others, the following, to be procured through any bookseller, are some of them the principal, and others of them amongst the principal, sources of information concerning the Over-taxation of Ireland :—

FINAL REPORT BY HER MAJESTY'S COMMISSIONERS APPOINTED TO ENQUIRE INTO THE FINANCIAL RELATIONS BETWEEN GREAT BRITAIN AND IRELAND. 228 pp., folio. *Price One Shilling and Ten Pence.* Eyre & Spottiswoode, London. This contains Mr. SEXTON'S Report and the other Reports enumerated in Introduction.

ENGLAND'S WEALTH, IRELAND'S POVERTY, by THOMAS LOUGH, M.P., with Ten Coloured Diagrams, 223, xv. pp. *Price One Shilling.* Downey & Co., York Street, Covent Garden, London.

ENGLAND'S DEBT TO IRELAND, by the late JAMES P. MAUNSELL, reprinted from the *Daily Express,* with Diagrams, 26 pp. *Price One Penny.* Office of the *Daily Express,* Dublin.

THE OVER-TAXATION OF IRELAND, a Record of City and County Meetings, the Declarations of Public Bodies, Chambers of Commerce, Political Conventions and British Statesmen, on the Financial Relations between Great Britain and Ireland, 292, xxii. pp. *Price One Shilling. Freeman's Journal* Company, Dublin.

THE FINANCIAL RELATIONS QUESTION, EXPENDITURE ACCOUNT, A Paper read before the Statistical Society of Ireland, by ARTHUR W. SAMUELS, Q.C. 32 pp. *Price Sixpence.* Sealy, Bryers & Walker, Dublin.

SOME FEATURES OF THE OVER-TAXATION OF IRELAND, A Paper read before the Statistical Society of Ireland, by NICHOLAS J. SYNNOTT, 20 pp. *Price Threepence.* Sealy, Bryers & Walker, Dublin.

www.ingramcontent.com/pod-product-compliance
Lightning Source LLC
Chambersburg PA
CBHW021529270326
41930CB00008B/1161